AF600329

RELIGIOUS ORDINARIES AND CANON 198

THE CATHOLIC UNIVERSITY OF AMERICA
CANON LAW STUDIES
No. 135

RELIGIOUS ORDINARIES AND CANON 198

A DISSERTATION

Submitted to the Faculty of Canon Law of the Catholic University of America in Partial Fulfillment of the Requirements for the Degree of Doctor of Canon Law

BY

MICHAEL JAMES KEENE, O.S.B.
Monk of the Abbey of St. Meinrad
Indiana

THE CATHOLIC UNIVERSITY OF AMERICA PRESS
WASHINGTON, D. C.
1942

IMPRIMI POTEST:

✠ Ignatius Esser, O.S.B.

Abbas Monasterii Sancti Meinradi

NIHIL OBSTAT:

Eduardus G. Roelker, S.T.D., J.C.D.

Censor Deputatus

IMPRIMATUR:

✠ Joseph E. Ritter, D.D.

Episcopus Indianapolitanus

Indianapoli, Ind., die XIV Julii, 1941

Printed by
The Abbey Press
St. Meinrad, Indiana

TO

MY FATHER AND MY MOTHER

TABLE OF CONTENTS

INTRODUCTION

Canon 198

§ 1: In iure nomine *Ordinarii* intelliguntur, nisi quis expresse excipiatur, praeter Romanum Pontificem, pro suo quisque territorio Episcopus residentialis, . . . pro suis vero subditis Superiores maiores in religionibus clericalibus exemptis.

§ 2: Nomine autem *Ordinarii loci* seu *locorum* veniunt omnes recensiti, exceptis Superioribus religiosis.*

The literal meaning of this canon as it stands in the Code seems to be sufficiently clear not to demand any further explanation. Since the text reads: "nisi quis expresse excipiatur," one could readily conclude that wherever the word *ordinary* occurs by itself it could always be substituted by the phrase *major superior of an exempt clerical religion.* If, however, one tries to apply that principle to the whole Code, he will meet with difficulties. One consults the best commentators on Canon Law and not infrequently finds that even these differ among themselves with regard to the exact meaning or extension of the canon. At other times they will agree that the canon under consideration can refer also to major superiors of exempt clerical religions, but only in such a way as not to exclude the influence and authority

* Woywod (*A Practical Commentary on the Code of Canon Law,* 75-76) gives the following translation of this canon: "By *Ordinaries* are to be understood in law (unless explicitly excepted in individual instances): the Roman Pontiff, within their respective territories the residential bishop, abbot and prelate *nullius* (and their vicar-general), administrator, vicar and prefect Apostolic. Furthermore, those persons are Ordinaries who, in case of vacancy of the above offices, succeed to the office during vacancy by the provisions of the law or of approved constitutions. In exempt clerical religious organizations, the major superiors are Ordinaries over their subjects. By the term *Ordinarius loci* or *locorum* are meant all persons enumerated in this Canon with the exception of the religious superiors."

of the ordinary of the place. For these reasons it is evident how advisable and useful a dissertation on this subject can be.

An investigation of the Code reveals the fact that the word *ordinary* standing alone and without any modifying determinative, such as "of the place" or "of the diocese," occurs 353 times in the Code (in 10 canons of Book I; in 57 canons of Book II; in 126 canons of Book III; in 105 canons of Book IV; and in 55 canons in Book V). However, in only 158 of these 353 instances can the word *ordinary* be judged as referring also to religious ordinaries. In the other 195 instances it must be interpreted in such a way as to exclude all those ordinaries who are not local ordinaries.

In order to avoid any confusion with regard to the treatment herein accorded to this subject, the writer deems it necessary at this particular point to declare definitely just what the purpose of this thesis is. He has chosen for consideration only the canons or the paragraphs in a canon which employ the word *ordinary* without any express indication as to whether it refers to both local and religious ordinaries or is restricted to the one or to the other as the case may be. The chief purpose of this thesis, therefore, is: To clarify and to understand more precisely to what extent the last part of paragraph one of canon 198 finds application in the entire Code.

In view of the assumption of the fundamental declaration: "In iure nomine Ordinarii intelliguntur . . . pro suis . . . subditis Superiores maiores in religionibus clericalibus exemptis," the question for each of the canons treated in this thesis may be formulated thus: Does or can the word *ordinary,* as delineated in canon 198, § 1, refer also to religious ordinaries? In order to arrive at a reasoned answer to that question the writer has relied upon and consulted the principal commentators of the Code. Whenever serious doubts arose as to the proper interpretation of any of the canons it has been found necessary to study not only post- but also pre-Code legislation.

The writer wishes to express his gratitude to the Right Reverend Ignatius Esser, O.S.B., Abbot of the Abbey of St. Meinrad, for the opportunity of graduate studies; to the Canon Law Faculty of the Pontifical Institute of Both Laws in Rome for help and guidance in his preparation especially for the degree of Licentiate in Canon Law; to the Canon Law Faculty at the Catholic University of America for suggestions, criticisms and generous assistance in the preparation of this study; and to all others who have in any way contributed to the completion of this dissertation.

CHAPTER I

EXPLANATION OF THE JURIDICAL MEANING OF THE TERMS: "ORDINARIES" AND "MAJOR SUPERIORS"

The first paragraph of canon 198 is clear in designating the persons who are juridically to be understood as ordinaries:

> **In iure nomine *Ordinarii* intelliguntur, nisi quis expresse excipiatur, praeter Romanum Pontificem, pro suo quisque territorio Episcopus residentialis, Abbas vel Praelatus *nullius* eorumque Vicarius Generalis, Administrator, Vicarius et Praefectus Apostolicus, itemque ii qui praedictis deficientibus interim ex iuris praescripto aut ex probatis constitutionibus succedunt in regimine, pro suis vero subditis Superiores maiores in religionibus clericalibus exemptis.**

The second paragraph of the same canon tells which of the above ordinaries are to be considered local ordinaries:

> **Nomine autem *Ordinarii loci* seu *locorum* veniunt omnes recensiti, exceptis Superioribus religiosis.**

Since the canon establishes the rule that all major superiors of clerical exempt religions are ordinaries, it is important to know just who are major superiors in religion. Canon 488, n. 8, is explicit on this point:

> **In canonibus qui sequuntur, veniunt nomine: 8°. *Superiorum maiorum*, Abbas Primas, Abbas Superior Congregationis monasticae, Abbas monasterii sui iuris, licet ad monasticam Congregationem pertinentis, supremus religionis Moderator, Superior provincialis, eorundem vicarii aliique ad instar provincialium potestatem habentes.**

In order to indicate more definitely which religious superiors are included under the designation *major superiors,* it has been thought advisable to define briefly each of the terms that occur in this canon.[1]

1.) *Major Superiors:* Very often the Code speaks of the highest superiors, the major superiors, and the minor superiors of a religion. Despite this, however, it explains precisely only the term *major superiors.* It does this because this term occurs much more frequently in the Code than the other two terms and because otherwise it would often be difficult to decide whether or not a certain superior is a major superior.

2.) *The abbot primate* (the abbot who presides over the confederation of the black Benedictines) *and the abbot general of a monastic Congregation* (abbot president, abbot superior, or superior general), even though they have not all the rights enjoyed by the other major superiors, yet juridically fall into the same category.[2]

3.) *The abbot of an exempt monastery:* Conventual priors in monastic congregations and superiors of exempt houses in centralized monastic religions both are to be considered as major superiors even as an abbot.

4.) *The supreme moderator of a religion and the provincial superior:* Although these may be called by various names, nevertheless in general there is no difficulty in distinguishing them.

5.) *The vicars of the same:* These words refer to all those named in canon 488, n. 8. Therefore it refers to the vicars of all those mentioned in the foregoing nn. 1, 2, 3, and 4.

6.) *And all others who have authority like to that of provincials:* Here are meant all those superiors who are not

---

[1] Cf. Arcadius Larraona, "Commentarium Codicis: Canon 488,"—*CpRM*, IV (1923), 39-46.

[2] Cf. canons 223, § 1, n. 4; 501, § 3; 510; 516, § 1; 655, § 1; 1579, § 2; and 1594, § 4.

provincials—either because the houses over which they preside for some reason or other do not form a moral person, or, if they do form a moral person, do not form a province according to the canonical sense of the word—but who nevertheless have authority like to that exercised by provincials, even though it may be in some ways restricted. In a like manner all canonical visitors who are constituted as such with an abiding capacity in a permanent office must be considered juridically as major superiors.

All superiors mentioned in the above six paragraphs, if they belong to a clerical exempt religion, must, therefore, be considered juridically as ordinaries.

CHAPTER II

FUNDAMENTAL NORMS

Thus far it has been determined just which religious superiors can be regarded as ordinaries in the technical, canonical sense of the word. Now there will be considered the two fundamental norms by means of which it can be determined to what extent in the individual canons these same superiors are included under the general designation of ordinaries.

A. First Fundamental Norm

> **In iure nomine ordinarii intelliguntur.... superiores Maiores in religionibus clericalibus exemptis.**[1]

In this text the law sets up the presumption that major superiors in clerical exempt religions are always included under the designation *ordinaries* wherever this term occurs unmodified in the Code. Henceforward if anyone should wish to exclude these superiors in the cases in which the Code speaks simply of ordinaries, he must first prove their exclusion, for on this point the juridical presumption stands in favor of the religious ordinary. Nevertheless, this principle must be used with discretion, for it is not without limitations. In fact these limitations, even in the Code itself, are very numerous, as has already been pointed out. In order to know when these limitations to the power of religious ordinaries are to be made, the two restrictions laid down by the Code for this principle must be kept in mind.

1. First Restriction: **Nisi quis expresse excipiatur.**[2]

This first restriction is very important, as is evident from the large number of cases in which the Code limits the

[1] Canon 198, § 1.

[2] Canon 198, § 1.

jurisdiction of religious ordinaries, either directly by excluding them,[3] or indirectly by granting only to local ordinaries jurisdiction with regard to certain matters.[4] A case in point is canon 1261, which constitutes the local ordinary as the official guardian of the public divine worship in all the territory committed to his charge. It is apropos here to quote this canon in full, since it so clearly establishes the authority of the local ordinary.

> **Canon 1261, § 1: Locorum Ordinarii advigilent ut sacrorum canonum prescripta de divino cultu sedulo observentur, et praesertim ne in cultum divinum sive publicum sive privatum aut in quotidianam fidelium vitam superstitiosa ulla praxis inducatur, aut quidquam admittatur a fide alienum vel ab ecclesiastica traditione absonum vel turpis quaestus speciem praeseferens.**
> **§ 2: Si loci Ordinarius leges pro suo territorio hac in re tulerit, etiam religiosi omnes, exempti quoque, obligatione tenentur easdem servandi; et Ordinarius potest eorundem ecclesias vel publica oratoria in hunc finem visitare.**

This exclusion of the jurisdiction of religious ordinaries may also be definitively indicated by an authentic interpretation of a previously doubtful canon[5] or by a subsequent law.

2. SECOND RESTRICTION: **Pro suis . . . subditis.**[6]

Religious ordinaries have jurisdiction only over their own subjects. Consequently, they will not be referred to when

---

[3] Cf. for example, canons 198, § 2 and 2253, n. 3.

[4] Cf. for example, canons 1261, §§ 1, 2 and 1999, § 3.

[5] Cf. for example, canon 883, § 1; the doubt concerning this canon was solved to the exclusion of religious ordinaries by the *Pontificia Commissio ad Codicis Canones Authentice Interpretandos*, July 30, 1934—*AAS*, XXVI (1934), 494; cf. also on this interpretation Maroto, "De Confessione Navigantium,"—*CpRM*, XV (1934), 356-358.

[6] Canon 198, § 1.

the Code speaks of affairs in which religious as religious do not enter. Thus the jurisdictional power of such superiors is excluded, for example, in all matters which treat of:

a.) the christian people as such; religious superiors have no authority, e.g., in matrimonial cases,[7] in legislation for the education of youth,[8] in conceding permission to preach in a diocese,[9] etc.

b.) or the diocesan clergy as such, as, for example, the titles XXVII, XXVIII, XXIX, XXX, XXXII of Book IV of the Code, concerning summary processes. It is clear that religious are not comprised in the legislation of these canons, for they presume that the parish priest has some right to a continued incumbency in his parish or benefice. He is either removable or irremovable. But a religious can never be considered even a "parochus amovibilis" in the same sense as a diocesan priest. The position of the religious is much less stable, so that at the mere will, either of the local ordinary or of his own superior, he can be removed from office.[10]

B. Second Fundamental Norm

In quo... ordinarii [loci] facultates minime privativae sunt, sed superior ius cumulativum cum ipso habet.[11]

---

[7] Canons 1012-1143.

[8] Canons 1372-1383, especially canon 1381.

[9] Canons 1337 and 1338.

[10] Canon 454, § 5.

[11] Canon 631, § 2. The entire paragraph reads as follows: "Ordinarius loci, ubi eum suo muneri defecisse compererit, opportuna decreta condere ac meritas in eum poenas statuere potest; in quo nihilominus Ordinarii facultates minime privativae sunt, sed Superior ius cumulativum cum ipso habet, ita tamen ut, si aliter a Superiore, aliter ab Ordinario decerni contingat, decretum Ordinarii praevalere debeat." Although the text of canon 631, § 2, considers religious simply in their capacity as parish priests, still by analogy the import of this text can be extended to include all religious who hold any office outside of the religious institute. Cf. also Benedictus XIV, const. *"Cum nuper"*, 8 nov. 1751, §§ 1, 4, and especially 5—*Fontes*, n. 417.

This second fundamental norm can be stated as follows: Religious superiors can punish their delinquent subjects not only when they have offended against their obligations as religious but also when they have offended against the obligations which they have by reason of an office which they hold outside of the religion, for example, as parish priests. This principle is a natural corollary of the dominative power which all religious superiors have over their subjects. But, as is quite evident, this principle cannot be twisted so as to obtain with equal effect for the local ordinary, for the latter has not any dominative power over these subjects. Juridically he can do nothing against an exempt religious who is delinquent *only* against his own proper obligations in religion, although he certainly has the power of correcting and, if need be, of punishing such a religious if the latter offends on any point in which he is subject to the local ordinary.[12]

The religious superior, however, must use prudence and good judgment in the exercise of this power, for even the natural law demands that he should not punish a religious who has already been punished *sufficiently* by the local ordinary. No one can justly be punished twice for the same delict. Still the principle must be acknowledged that the superior can punish a religious even after he has been punished by the local ordinary, provided that, in the superior's prudent judgment, the subject has not been punished sufficiently, or provided that, apart from such added pun-

[12] Thus canon 619: "In omnibus in quibus religiosi subsunt Ordinario loci, possunt ab eodem etiam poenis coerceri." And canon 631, § 1: "Idem parochus vel vicarius religiosus, licet ministerium exerceat in domo seu loco ubi maiores Superiores religiosi ordinariam sedem habent, subest immediate omnimodae iurisdictioni, vistationi, et correctioni Ordinarii loci, non secus ac parochi saeculares, regulari observantia unice excepta." Cf. Benedictus XIV, const. "*Firmandis*," 6 nov. 1744, § 10—*Fontes*, n. 349; also Goyeneche, "Consultationes," —*CpRM*, X (1929), 181 and Noval, *Commentarium Codicis Iuris Canonici*, Liber IV, *De Processibus*, Pars I, *De Iudiciis* (Augustae Taurinorum—Romae: Marietti, 1920), 494. Hereafter this work will be referred to as *De Iudiciis*.

ishment, scandal could not be avoided in the religious house itself.

This second norm may seem to be only a corollary of the first norm, but it is more. Although it flows from the dominative power common to all religious superiors, yet it has this relation to jurisdictional power: it states more clearly the extent to which the superior's jurisdiction can be exercised.

If despite the application of the two norms here expressed any doubts still remain as to the interpretation of one or the other of the canons in the Code, they will have to be solved according to the sound principles of interpretation as laid down in Book I of the Code.

On the basis of the above principles the entire Code has been studied with the following result: the word *ordinary* without modification occurs in the Code 353 times, of which in 158 canons it can be interpreted as including also religious ordinaries, while in the other 195 canons it must be interpreted as connoting their exclusion. In the following pages, after an enumeration of the canons which fall into the one or the other category, there will be a discussion of those canons relative to which there may exist some doubt concerning their applicable reference to or implicit inclusion of major religious superiors under the term *ordinary* in view particularly of the doctrine presented by commentators on certain moot questions.

CHAPTER III

CANONS IN WHICH THE WORD "ORDINARY" DOES REFER ALSO TO RELIGIOUS ORDINARIES*

FIRST BOOK
Can. 5[1]
15[2]
36, § 1[3]
44, § 1[4]
47[5]
51[6]
61[7]
66, § 2[8]
78[9]
81[10]

SECOND BOOK
Can. 127[14]
128[15]
139, §§ 3 & 4[17]
141, § 1[18]
149[20]
157[21]
188, nn. 2,7,8[22]
192, § 3[24]
198, § 1[25]
239, n. 22[27]
247, § 4[28]
269, §§ 2 & 3
274, n. 5[29]
696, § 2[30]

THIRD BOOK
Can. 838[31]
841, § 1[32]
843, § 2[33]
880, § 2[35]
968, § 1[38]
972, § 1[39]
984, n. 3[40]
987, nn. 6 & 7[41]
990, §§ 1 & 2[42]
994, § 2[43]
999[45]
1001, §§ 1 & 2[46]
1010, § 2[47]
1151, §§ 1 & 2[48]
1157[49]
1164, § 1[50]
1165, § 2[51]
1169, § 4[52]
1176, § 3[53]
1179[54]
1183, § 2[55]
1185
1191, § 2[56]
1192, §§ 1-4[57]
1193[58]
1195, §§ 1 & 2[59]
1200, § 1[60]
1201, § 3[61]
1214, §§ 1 & 2[62]
1240, § 2[63]

---

* In the enumeration of the canons, the numbers found after the various canons refer to the notes and comments found in chapter V beginning on page 15.

1245, § 2[64]
1279, § [65]
1280[66]
1303, § 2[67]
1341, § 1[68]
1342, § 1[69]
1363, § 1[72]
1378
1397, § 5[73]
1401[74]
1402, § 1[75]
1403, § 1[76]
1406, § 1, n. 8[77]
1503[80]
1515, §§ 1,2,3[82]
1516, §§ 1,2,3[83]
1517, § 2[84]
1523, n. 4[86]
1536, § 2[87]
1538, § 2[88]
1539, § 2[89]
1547

FOURTH BOOK

Can. 1562, §§ 1 & 2[92]
1580, §§ 1 & 2[93]
1585, § 2[94]
1589, § 1[96]
1599, § 1, n. 1[97]
1601[98]
1614, § 2[99]
1615, §§ 2 & 3[100]
1621, § 1[101]
1648, § 3[102]
1649[103]
1651, §§ 1 & 2[104]
1658, §§ 1 & 2[105]
1665, § 2
1813, § 1, n. 1 & 4[106]
1939, § 1[107]
1942, § 1[108]
1946, §§ 1 & 2[108]
1947[109]
1948, n. 3[109]
1950[109]
1951, § 2[109]
1956
1994, § 1[110]
2144, § 2[111]
2145, § 1[111]
2146, § 3[111]
2176[112]
2177[112]
2178[112]
2179[112]
2180[112]
2186[113]
2187[113]
2188[113]
2189[113]
2190[113]
2191[113]
2193[113]
2194[113]

FIFTH BOOK

Can. 2214, § 2
2237, §§ 1 & 2[114]
2245, § 2
2247, § 1
2253, n. 3
2293, § 3
2295
2301[115]
2302[115]
2307

2308
2309, § 3
2311, § 1
2313, § 2
2317
2321[117]
2322, n. 2
2323
2324
2325
2326
2329[118]
2331, §§ 1 & 2
2337, §§ 1 & 2[119]
2339
2341
2342, n. 1[120]
2343, § 4
2344
2346
2348
2350, §§ 1 & 2
2357, § 1
2361
2364
2380
2383
2388, §§ 1 & 2
2391, § 2
2394, n. 1
2399
2406, §§ 1 & 2

CHAPTER IV

CANONS IN WHICH THE WORD "ORDINARY" DOES NOT REFER TO RELIGIOUS ORDINARIES*

SECOND BOOK

Can. 94, §§ 1 & 2[11]
114[12]
116[12]
117, §§ 2 & 3[12]
126[13]
136, § 3[16]
143[19]
192, § 2[23]
239, nn. 15 & 18[26]
248, § 3
250, § 2
261
281
292, §§ 2 & 3
376, § 2
378, § 1
406, § 2
421, § 1, n. 2
454, § 5
458
465, §§ 2,4,5
470, §§ 1 & 4
471, § 3
473, § 2
475, § 3
476, §§ 1, 4-7
480, § 1
488, n. 3
492, § 2
495, §§ 1 & 2
497, § 3
506, § 2
514, § 3
520, § 2
521, § 2
524, § 1
525
526
529
535, § 1, n. 2
622, § 4
631, § 2
671, nn. 2 & 6

THIRD BOOK

Can. 729, n. 2
735
783, § 1
784
785, § 3
804, § 1
848, § 2[34]
883, § 1[36]
899, § 3[37]
929
960

* In the enumeration of the canons, the numbers found after the various canons refer to the notes and comments found in chapter V beginning on page 15.

979, § 2
981, § 2
998, §§ 1 & 3[44]
1000, §§ 1 & 2[44]
1023, § 2
1028, § 2
1031
1055
1063, § 2
1064
1065, § 2
1066
1091
1098
1102, § 2
1103, § 1
1105
1106
1109, §§ 2 & 3
1122, § 1
1131, § 2
1132
1162, § 2
1171
1186, n. 2
1218, § 2
1232, § 1
1233, § 1
1263, § 3
1279, §§ 2 & 3[65]
1333, § 2
1338, § 1
1344, §§ 2 & 3[70]
1346, § 2
1349, § 1[71]
1393, § 4
1394, § 1
1414, § 2[78]
1415, § 2[78]
1417, § 1[78]
1424[78]
1426[78]
1427, §§ 1,3,4[78]
1428, § 3[78]
1430, § 1[78]
1432, § 3[78]
1444, § 1[78]
1453, § 2[79]
1458, § 2[79]
1459, § 2[79]
1464, §§ 2 & 3[79]
1465, § 1[79]
1466, § 3[79]
1469[79]
1470, § 1, n. 4[79]
1484[78]
1485[78]
1486[78]
1487, § 2[78]
1506[81]
1519, § 2[85]
1520, §§ 1 & 4
1541, § 2, n. 3[90]

FOURTH BOOK

Can. 1586[95]
1734
1923, § 2
1933, § 3
1979, § 2
1990
2002
2011, § 2
2025, §§ 1,2,3
2037, § 2

2038, § 2
2039, § 2
2040, §§ 1 & 2
2043, § 1
2044, § 1
2046
2047, § 1
2049
2056, § 2
2063, §§ 1 & 3
2064
2075
2082
2084
2085
2086, §§ 1 & 3
2088, § 1
2092
2126
2127
2147 to 2156
2158 to 2161
2162 to 2167
2168 to 2175
2180
2181
2182
2183
2184
2185

FIFTH BOOK

Can. 2303, § 2[116]
2304, § 1[116]
2319, § 1
2347, n. 2[121]
2349
2356
2373, n. 1[122]
2375
2376
2377
2381, n. 1
2382
2405

CHAPTER V

COMMENTARY ON THE INDIVIDUAL CANONS

A. Commentary on Book I

In Book I of the Code, as has been seen, there are ten instances in which the word *ordinary* occurs without modification. In all of these cases religious ordinaries are meant as well as local ordinaries. In general, authors sedulously keep canon 198 in mind when commenting on Book I and therefore explicitly state that religious ordinaries are included, or are not included, as the case may be.

1. Canon 5:

> **Vigentes in praesens contra horum statuta canonum consuetudines sive universales sive particulares, si quidem ipsis canonibus expresse *reprobentur*, tanquam iuris corruptelae corrigantur, licet sint immemorabiles, neve sinantur in posterum reviviscere; aliae, quae quidem centenariae sint et immemorabiles, tolerari poterunt, si Ordinarii pro locorum ac personarum adiunctis existiment eas prudenter submoveri non posse; ceterae suppressae habeantur, nisi expresse Codex aliud caveat.**

This canon gives to all ordinaries the permission to tolerate any contrary centenary or immemorial custom provided that it is not expressly condemned or reprobated in the Code and provided, likewise, that the ordinary seriously judges that it would not be prudent to abolish it. With regard to the application of this canon authors in large numbers state that not only local ordinaries but also major superiors of exempt clerical religions are meant whenever there is question of a custom affecting an order or a religious province.[1]

[1] Capello, *Summa Iuris Canonici* (3 vols., Romae: Apud Aedes Universitatis Gregorianae, Vols. I-II, 3. ed., 1938-1939; Vol. III, 1936),

Against the authors who hold this opinion the seeming restriction of Ayrinhac[2] cannot be sustained. By omitting all reference to religious ordinaries and by substituting the term *ordinary of the place* for the more comprehensive term *ordinary* which is used in the text of the Code, he appears to consider this canon as not applicable to religious ordinaries. He writes: "Customs not mentioned in any way and contrary to some provisions of the Code, whether they be universal or particular, are abrogated unless they have existed from time immemorial, in which case the Ordinary of the place may tolerate them if, considering local and personal circumstances, he judges that they could not prudently be abolished." Since Ayrinhac gives no reasons for such an opinion, the above wording in his commentary is evidently not fully considered or deliberately intended to exclude religious ordinaries. The author simply takes into consideration only local ordinaries and proceeds according-

---

I, 61; cf. also Berutti, *Institutiones Iuris Canonici* (3 vols., Taurini: Marietti, 1936), I, 5; Beste, *Introductio in Codicem* (Collegeville, Minn., St. John's Abbey Press, 1938), p. 73; Blat, *Normae Generales* (Romae, 1921), p. 66; Claeys Bouuaert-Simenon, *Manuale Iuris Canonici* (3 vols., Gandae et Leodii: Prostat apud Auctores in Seminariis Gandavensi et Leodiensi, Vols. I and III, 4. ed., 1934; Vol. II, 2. ed., 1935), I, 87, note 1; Cicognani, *Canon Law* (authorized English Version by J. O'Hara and F. Brennan, 2. ed., Philadelphia: The Dolphin Press, 1935), p. 489; Coronata, *Institutiones Iuris Canonici* (5 vols., Romae: Marietti, Vols. I-II, 2. ed., 1939; Vol. III, 1933; Vol. IV, 1935; Vol. V, 1936), I, 8; Goyeneche, *Juris Canonici Summa Principia* (Romae: Tip. Pol. "Cuore di Maria," 1935), p. 63; Michiels, *Normae Generales Juris Canonici* (2 vols., Lublin: Universitas Catholica, 1929), I, 81; Mothon, *Traité sur L'État Religieux* (Paris, 1922), p. 55; Schaefer, *De Religiosis* (3. ed., Romae: Herder, 1940), p. 701; Sipos, *Enchiridion Iuris Canonici,* (3. ed., Pecs: Ex Typographia "Haladas R. T.," 1936), p. 28; Vermeersch-Creusen, *Epitome Iuris Canonici* (3 vols., Mechliniae: H. Dessain, Vol. I, 6. ed., 1937; Vol. II, 5. ed., 1934; Vol. III, 5. ed., 1936), I, 72; Wernz-Vidal, *Ius Canonicum* (7 toms. in 8 vols., Romae: Apud Aedes Universitatis Gregorianae, 1923-1938), I, 130.

[2] *General Legislation in the New Code of Canon Law* (New York: Longmans, 1933), p. 105.

ly. Since that was his intention, what he writes is in itself not wrong, although it is misleading, for canon 5 certainly includes all those who, according to canon 198, § 1, fall under the term *ordinary*. Ayrinhac, however, is not alone in this oversight. It was made also and seemingly for the same reason by a French writer, Couly, in an article in *Le Canoniste.*[3]

2. Canon 15:

> **Leges, etiam irritantes et inhabilitantes, in dubio iuris non urgent; in dubio autem facti potest ordinarius in eis dispensare, dummodo agatur de legibus in quibus Romanus Pontifex dispensare solet.**

A like uniformity of doctrine is had with regard to this canon. Whenever there is question of a doubt with regard to a fact, all ordinaries can dispense from laws in which the Roman Pontiff is wont to grant dispensations. Expressing the common opinion of the authors Vermeersch-Creusen write that, according to the different matter and the various persons under consideration, the ordinary will be either the local or the religious ordinary.[4]

---

[3] "Le Coutûme en Droit Canonique,"—*Le Canoniste*, XLVIII (1926), 441; the same omission is noticed in Guilfoyle, *Custom* (The Catholic University of America, Canon Law Studies, n. 105, Washington, D. C.: The Catholic University of America, 1937), pp. 73 ff.

[4] *Epitome*, I, 108; cf. also Berutti, *Institutiones*, I, 82; Blat, *Normae Generales*, p. 93; Claeys Bouuart-Simenon, *Manuale*, I, 93; Cappello, *Summa Iuris Canonici*, I, 139; Cicognani, *Canon Law*, p. 589; Coronata, *Institutiones*, I, 32; Michiels, *Normae Generales*, I, 337; Mothon, *Institutions Canoniques* (3 vols., Paris, 1922), I, 16; H. Noldin-Schmitt, *Summa Theologiae Moralis Iuxta Codicem Iuris Canonici* (3 vols., 24. ed., Oeniponte: F. Rauch, 1936), I, 185; Schaefer, *De Religiosis*, p. 236; Toso, *Ad Codicem Iuris Canonici Commentaria Minora* (5 vols., Romae: Marietti, 1920-1934), I, 36; Van Hove, *De Legibus Ecclesiasticis* (Mechliniae-Romae: H. Dessain, 1930), p. 237; Wernz-Vidal, *Ius Canonicum*, I, 471; Eichmann, *Lehrbuch des Kirchenrechts* (2. ed., Paderborn, 1926), p. 68; Fanfani, *De Iure Religiosorum ad Normam Codicis Iuris Canonici* (2. ed., Augustae Taurinorum, 1925), p. 68.

3. Canon 36, § 1:

Rescripta tum Sedis Apostolicae tum aliorum Ordinariorum impetrari libere possunt ab omnibus qui expresse non prohibentur.

Major superiors of exempt clerical religions can give rescripts in the technical sense in which this word is understood by the Code. Claeys Bouuaert-Simenon point out that this is a new development brought in by the Code since before the Code the word *rescript* was reserved to responses sent out by the Holy See. Now, however, it applies also to favors granted by all ordinaries.[5] Wernz, writing in 1913, testified to the rule that ecclesiastical rescripts in the strict sense of the word could be granted by the Roman Pontiff alone.[6]

4. Canon 44, § 1:

Nemo gratiam a proprio Ordinario denegatam ab alio Ordinario petat, nulla facta denegationis mentione; facta autem mentione, Ordinarius gratiam ne concedat, nisi habitis a priore Ordinario denegationis rationibus.

In this canon it is stated that no one, after having been denied a favor by his own ordinary, should, without mentioning this fact, ask the same favor of another ordinary. Furthermore, the second ordinary should not grant the favor without first having taken cognizance of the reasons underlying the refusal of the first ordinary. Coronata gives a very complete enumeration of the various proper ordi-

---

[5] *Manuale*, I, 115: "... a quocumque Ordinario..."; cf. also Berutti, *Institutiones*, I, 122; Beste, *Introductio in Codicem*, p. 106; Blat, *Normae Generales*, p. 128; Coronata, *Institutiones*, I, 70; Vermeersch-Creusen, *Epitome*, I, 141.

[6] *Ius Decretalium ad usum Praelectionum in Scholis Textus Iuris Canonici sive Iuris Decretalium* (6 toms. in 10 vols., Prati, Tom. I, 3. ed., 1913; Tom. II, pars. 1, 2, 3. ed., 1915; Tom. III, pars. 1, 2, 2. ed. [Romae], 1908; Tom. IV, pars. 1, 2, 2. ed., 1911-1912; Tom. V, pars. 1, 2, 1914; Tom. VI, 1914), Tom. I, n. 150.

naries who can be affected by this canon: e.g., if one should have many domiciles or quasi-domiciles; if in the same place there should be more than one superior and each should have authority by virtue of a different jurisdiction, as for example the local ordinary and a legate of the Holy See (the one has ordinary power and the other delegated); for religious the ordinary will be either the supreme or major superior and, with regard to certain matters, also the local ordinary; finally there can be the ordinary of the place where one has his domicile and the ordinary of the place in which one happens to be as a stranger.[7]

Mothon[8] declares that this canon holds with equal efficacy in the case of a religious asking for a favor from the Holy See after it has been refused by his own proper ordinary. This, however, is most certainly an extensive interpretation and cannot, therefore, be authentically declared by any private authority. Especially is this the case since canon 44

---

[7] *Institutiones*, I, 77; cf. also Ayrinhac, *General Legislation*, p. 151; Berutti, *Institutiones*, I, 134-135; Blat, *Normae Generales*, p. 137; Claeys Bouuaert-Simenon, *Manuale*, I, 118; Cappello, *Summa Iuris Canonici*, I, 165; Cicognani, *Canon Law*, p. 724; Cocchi, *Commentarium in Codicem Iuris Canonici* (8 vols., Taurinorum Augustae: Marietti, Vol. I, 5. ed., 1938; Vol. II, 4. ed., 1937; Vol. III, 3. ed., 1931; Vols. IV-V, 3. ed., 1932; Vol. VI, 3. ed., 1933; Vol. VII, 3. ed., 1940; Vol. VIII, 4. ed., 1938), I, 252; Maroto, *Institutiones iuris Canonici ad Normam Novi Codicis* (2 vols., Romae, Vol. I, 3. ed., 1921; Vol. II, 1919), I, 323; Michiels, *Normae Generales*, II, 182; Oesterle, *Praelectiones Iuris Canonici* (Romae: Apud Collegium S. Anselmi, 1931), p. 28; Van Hove, *De Rescriptis* (Mechliniae-Romae: H. Dessain, 1936), p. 163; Vermeersch-Creusen, *Epitome*, I, 144; Wernz-Vidal, *Ius Canonicum*, I, 406.

[8] *Institutions Canoniques*, I, 500: "Dans tous les ordres, ou congrégations, de l'un ou l'autre sexe, aucune grâce, ou permission, ne peut être sollicitée du supérieur, ou de la supérieure majeure, qui a été auparavant refusée par le supérieur, ou la supérieure intermédiare, à moins qu'on ne fasse connaître au supérieur, ou à la supérieure majeure, le refus du supérieur, ou de la supérieure intermédiaire. Cette règle canonique s'applique également dans le cas ou les religieux et religieuses en appellent de leurs supérieurs religieux au Saint-Siège."

is a law restricting the free use of a natural right. Consequently, in accord with the principle of interpretation as laid down in canon 19, it must be strictly interpreted.[9]

It is true that this restriction does not in any event bind under pain of consequent nullity.[10] Although it may readily be admitted that one who has been refused by his own proper ordinary should not ask for the same favor from the Holy See without mentioning that fact, it cannot be said that such a person acts illicitly if he acts contrariwise. Such a restriction is nowhere stated in the Code and hence it cannot be upheld as a law.[11]

On the other hand, the Holy See does not act beyond its authority if it grants the favor despite the refusal of the ordinary. A further confirmatory argument for this last statement is had in the wording of canon 43, for it says that a favor, refused by one Sacred Congregation or Office of the Roman Curia, without such a Congregation's or Office's consent, simply cannot be granted by any other Office or Congregation or by a local ordinary. Any attempts to grant would be futile for the concession would be invalid. It is to be noted that the canon deals with a favor which has been denied by a Roman Congregation or Office, but makes no reference to a favor which has been refused by any inferior authority, as, for example, by an ordinary. From this noticeable omission it is logical to conclude that the Holy See is in no way bound by the refusal of a favor by any ordinary.

This is the conclusion which must be reached when studying the matter academically. Practically, however, there will be no difficulty with regard to this point since the Holy See is accustomed to promote good discipline and order by granting favors *through* the proper ordinaries. Hence if the Holy See in some particular instance sees fit

---

[9] Cf. Michiels, *Normae Generales*, II, 182.

[10] Cf. canon 11 and also Ferreres, *Institutiones Canonicae* (Barcinonae, 1920), I, 82.

[11] Cf. Beste, *Introductio in Codicem*, p. 110.

to grant a favor which has already been refused by the petitioner's own immediate ordinary, it will grant the favor through that ordinary and thereby preserve his full authority.

5. **Canon 47:**

> **Rescripta non fiunt irrita ob errorem in nomine personae cui vel a qua conceduntur, aut loci in quo ipsa moratur, aut rei de qua agitur, dummodo, iudicio Ordinarii, nulla sit de ipsa persona vel re dubitatio.**

Rescripts are not rendered void because of incidental errors regarding the names of persons, places, or things provided that, in the judgment of the ordinary, there is no real doubt with regard to the precise persons, places, or things designated. "In case of doubt, it is for the Ordinary of the place in which the rescript is to be used, or for the personal superior if the petitioners are Religious enjoying the privilege of exemption, to judge whether the petition is sufficiently definite in spite of errors."[12]

6. **Canon 51:**

> **Rescriptum Sedis Apostolicae in quo nullus datur exsecutor, tunc tantum debet Ordinario impetrantis praesentari, cum id in eisdem litteris praecipitur, aut de rebus agitur publicis, aut comprobare conditiones quasdam oportet.**

A rescript of the Apostolic See in which no executor is appointed need not be presented to the ordinary of the petitioner unless this is required in the rescript itself, or there is question of public affairs, or it is an affair in which

---

[12] Thus Ayrinhac, *General Legislation*, p. 148; the following authors express the same opinion: Berutti, *Institutiones*, I, 137; Coronata, *Institutiones*, I, 79; Cappello, *Summa Iuris Canonici*, I, 172; Maroto, *Institutiones*, I, 318; Oesterle, *Praelectiones Iuris Canonici*, p. 31; *Vermeersch-Creusen*, *Epitome*, I, 148.

the ordinary must examine certain conditions. Van Hove expresses the common opinion when he says that by the word *ordinary* in this canon are meant also major superiors of clerical exempt religions. In a footnote he adds that these rescripts must be presented to the religious ordinary when there is question of matters in which the religious enjoy exemption from the local ordinary. On the other hand, religious must present such rescripts to the diocesan ordinary in all cases in which they are subject to his jurisdiction.[13] Ordinarily, as Augustine notes, the rescripts which concern religious must be presented to their own superior who, in the case of exempt clerical religious, is himself the ordinary.[14]

7. Canon 61:

> **Per Apostolicae Sedis aut dioecesis vacationem nullum eiusdem Sedis Apostolicae aut Ordinarii rescriptum perimitur, nisi aliud ex additis clausulis appareat, aut rescriptum contineat potestatem alicui factam concedendi gratiam peculiaribus personis in eodem expressis, et res adhuc integra sit.**

Since the Code says that during the vacancy of the Holy See or of a diocese no rescript of the same Holy See or of the ordinary loses its authority, authors are somewhat chary about expressly including religious ordinaries under the word *ordinary* in this canon. As is evident, if one considers the words alone, there is no explicit and direct reference to religious ordinaries in this canon. Nevertheless, though one must fully grant the correctness of this statement, one can simultaneously advert to the slight *lacuna* in

---

[13] Van Hove, *De Rescriptis*, p. 218 and note 4; for a like interpretation cf.: Berutti, *Institutiones*, I, 142; Blat, *Normae Generales*, p. 144; Coronata, *Institutiones*, I, 84; Michiels, *Normae Generales*, II, 264, note 3.

[14] *Rights and Duties of Ordinaries* (St. Louis: B. Herder, 1924), p. 109.

the law and in consequence thereof bridge over the gap, so that through the application of canon 20 one may by analogy regard the rule of canon 61 as applying also in the cases wherein rescripts were granted by religious ordinaries. Therefore these rescripts also continue in force during the vacancy of the offices in which the religious ordinaries were the incumbents.

Another reason for this opinion is found in the principle which is invoked by canon 73 regarding the continuance of privileges. All rescripts are considered as having been granted permanently unless the contrary is proved.[15] This rule holds, therefore, not only for the rescripts which are granted by local ordinaries, but also for all other rescripts which are granted by a competent ecclesiastical authority.

8. **Canon 66, § 2:**

> **Nisi in earum concessione electa fuerit industria personae aut aliud expresse cautum sit, facultates habituales, Episcopo aliisve de quibus in can. 198, § 1 ab Apostolica Sede concessae, non evanescunt, resoluto iure Ordinarii cui concessae sunt, etiamsi ipse eas exsequi coeperit, sed transeunt ad Ordiarios qui ipsi in regimine succedunt; item concessae Episcopo competunt quoque Vicario Generali.**

Unless they contain a direct statement to the contrary, or were given to a definite individual because of his personal qualifications, the habitual faculties which are granted by the Apostolic See to the bishop or to others mentioned in canon 198, § 1, do not become inoperative with the lapse from office of the ordinary to whom they were given, but pass on to the succeeding ordinary. The strongest argument for the inclusion of religious ordinaries in this paragraph is found in the wording of the very text of the Code:

[15] Cf. Michiels, *Normae Generales*, II, 299: "Ratio est, quia rescripta omnia ex benevolentia principis censentur regulariter in perpetuum elargita (can. 73)." Of the same opinion are: Berutti, *Institutiones*, I, 151; and Cappello, *Summa Iuris Canonici*, I, 181.

aliisve de quibus in can. 198,§ 1, for religious ordinaries are also meant without any doubt in canon 198.

Roelker, commenting on canon 66, § 2, writes: "The general principle to be followed, then, is that habitual faculties do not cease with their grantee's loss of power. The Code refers to the list of those whose faculties enjoy this continuance. Canon 198, § 1, states who are the Ordinaries in the law. Besides the Roman Pontiff, such Ordinaries are residential Bishops, Abbots and Prelates *nullius*, together with Vicars General, Administrators, Vicars and Prefects Apostolic. All these are *Ordinarii locorum.* In addition to these Ordinaries are to be considered the Major Superiors of exempt clerical religious."[16] Moreover habitual faculties granted to ordinaries have the nature of real privileges which pertain to the office rather than to the person; consequently they automatically pass on to whatever person administers the office, no matter by what name he may be called.[17]

9. Canon 78:

Qui abutitur potestate sibi ex privilegio permissa, privilegio ipso privari meretur; et Ordinarius Sanctam Sedem monere ne omittat, si quis privilegio ab eadem concesso graviter abutatur.

---

[16] Roelker, *Principles of Privilege according to the Code of Canon Law* (The Catholic University of America, Canon Law Studies, n. 35, Washington, D. C.: The Catholic University of America, 1926), p. 149; cf. also Ayrinhac, *General Legislation*, p. 176; Berutti, *Institutiones*, I, 160-161; Beste, *Introductio in Codicem*, p. 121; Biederlack-Führich, *De Religiosis* (Oeniponte, 1919), p. 260; Blat, *Normae Generales*, p. 163; Claeys Bouuaert-Simenon, *Manuale*, I, 129; Cance, *Le Code de Droit Canonique* (3 vols., Paris, 1927-1929), I, 98; Cappello, *Summa Iuris Canonici*, I, 196; Cocchi, *Commentarium*, I, 269; Maroto, *Institutiones*, I, 348; Mothon, *Traité sur L'État Religieux*, p. 48; Van Hove, *De Privilegiis* (Mechliniae-Romae: H. Dessain, 1930), p. 157; Vermeersch-Creusen, *Epitome*, I, 158; Wernz-Vidal, *Ius Canonicum*, I, 435.

[17] Cf. Chelodi, *Ius de Personis* (2. ed. a Sac. Ernesto Bertagnolli recognita et aucta, Tridenti, Libr. Edit. Tridentum, 1927), p. 146.

This canon states that the ordinary should inform the Holy See about the abuse of any privilege granted by the same Holy See. The reason is obvious. Otherwise such abuses would for the most part never come to the notice of the Holy See. Roelker puts the matter succinctly: "In the matter of Papal privileges, the Code demands that Ordinaries advise the Holy See of abuses of privileges. All Superiors who come under the name 'Ordinary' are included."[18]

Canon 617, § 1, treats directly of the question of an abuse of a privilege by an exempt religious and imposes on the local ordinary the obligation of referring the matter to the Holy See if, after he has warned the religious superior, the latter does nothing to remedy the abuse.[19]

10. Canon 81:

> **A generalibus Ecclesiae legibus Ordinarii infra Romanum Pontificem dispensare nequeunt, ne in casu quidem peculiari, nisi haec potestas eisdem fuerit explicite vel implicite concessa, aut nisi difficilis sit recursus ad Sanctam Sedem et simul in mora sit periculum gravis damni, et de dispensatione agatur quae a Sede Apostolica concedi solet.**

By this canon ordinaries are given the power to dispense from the general rules of the Church provided that recourse to Rome is difficult, provided that there is danger of a serious harm or detriment should there be any delay in the

[18] *Principles of Privilege*, p. 131; Cf. also S. C. de Prop. Fide, decr. 13 aug. 1774—*Fontes*, n. 4567; Blat, *Normae Generales*, p. 171; Michiels, *Normae Generales*, II, 420; and Berutti, *Institutiones*, I, 167: "Ab antiquitus hoc principium viget in iure canonico, quod etiam urgendum in praxi pluries a S. Sede statutum est........; quoties proinde scandalum seu damnum fidelibus causetur ob privilegii abusum quod ab Apostolica Sede concessum fuerit, quum Ordinarius loci et Ordinarius religiosorum proprios subditos praefato privilegio ipsi directe et immediate privare nequeant, iidem obligatione tenentur abusum denuntiandi S. Sedi ut ipsa congrua provideat."

[19] Cf. Van Hove, *De Privilegiis*, p. 285.

granting of the dispensation and, thirdly, provided that there is question of a dispensation which the Holy See ordinarily grants. All three of these conditions must be fulfilled before the ordinary can grant such a dispensation. Nearly all authors expressly uphold this power for religious ordinaries as well as for local ordinaries. Cicognani, to cite only one example, has the following: "Under the term 'Ordinaries,' spoken of in canon 81, should be included the Superiors or Moderators General of Religious institutes in matters which their rule or constitutions have taken over from the common law, but not with respect to those matters which, though peculiar to an Institute, have nonetheless been approved by the Holy See and made of Pontifical right. It should be noted, however, that authorities on the Law of Religious commonly held—and their opinion still seems tenable under the Code—that Religious Prelates unless expressly forbidden enjoy tacit power of *dispensing with discretion* from the prescriptions of their rule *in a particular case*. Right government would seem to require this; and of course this faculty is restricted *to those minor observances* which do not pertain to the substance of religion. What these may be, custom, 'the best expounder of laws', will decide. Thus, for instance, a Superior cannot dispense from the second year of the novitiate, where it is required; nor from holding General Chapters at the required times; besides, these cases can be foreseen, and timely recourse to the Holy See can easily be had. The contrary is true if in virtue of the constitutions themselves or of a special privilege a Superior before the Code had power to dispense, for in a given case he can also dispense today according to the rule of canons 4 and 489. On this point Suarez states that authors hold it to be a general rule that all Religious Prelates in the matter of dispensing can do only that which is accorded them by law or privilege, or by their rule."[20]

---

[20] Cicognani, *Canon Law*, 839-840; cf. also Aertnys-Damen, *Theologia Moralis* (2 vols., 13. ed., Taurini: Marietti, 1939), I, 704; Augustine, *Rights and Duties of Ordinaries*, p. 122; Berutti, *Institu-*

According to canon 81, therefore, all ordinaries[21] can dispense from the general laws of the Church only: 1.) If that power has been explicitly granted to them: This power has been explicitly granted in the Code to all ordinaries in the following cases: canons 15; 972, § 1; 990, § 1; 1245, § 2; 1313 and 1320; 2.) If that power has been implicitly granted to them: This power of dispensing is granted implicitly when the law contains the words: "nisi dispensatum fuerit," "donec dispensetur," "dispensari posse," or some other similar phrase. By such words the power to dispense is granted to ordinaries. Otherwise there would be no need for the phrase at all since no one doubts that the Holy Father can dispense from such laws. Moreover, there seems to be no reason to restrict to local ordinaries this power granted by implicit concession, although, of course, each ordinary's power is limited to the extent of his jurisdiction over persons and things;[22] 3.) Or in an

---

tiones, I, 172; Beste, *Introductio in Codicem,* p. 126; Blat, *Normae Generales,* p. 176; Claeys Bouuaert-Simenon, *Manuale,* I, 134; Cance, *Le Code de Droit Canonique,* I, 107, note 1; Cappello, *Summa Iuris Canonici,* I, 136, note 8; Chelodi, *Ius de Personis,* p. 155; Cocchi, *Commentarium,* I, 291; Eichmann, *Lehrbuch des Kirchenrechts,* p. 68; Goyeneche, "Consultationes,"—*CpRM,* XIX (1938), 161-163 and III (1922), 54-57; Mayer, *Benediktinisches Ordensrecht in der Beuroner Kongregation* (4 vols., Hohenzollern: Kunstverlag Beuron, 1929-1936), II, 180 and III, 299; Michiels, *Normae Generales,* II, 480; Mothon, *Institutions Canoniques,* I, 16 and *Traité sur L'État Religieux,* p. 41; Reilly, *The General Norms of Dispensation* (The Catholic University of America, Canon Law Studies, n. 119, Washington, D. C.: The Catholic University of America Press, 1939), 65-66; Schaefer, *De Religiosis,* p. 236; Toso, *Commentaria Minora,* I, 176; Van Hove, *De Privilegiis,* p. 368; Vermeersch-Creusen, *Epitome,* I, 168; Wernz-Vidal, *Ius Canonicum,* I, 471 and III, 112; Brys, "Explicatio Canonis 81,"—*Collationes Brugenses,* XXIX (1929), 145-146; Coronata, *Institutiones,* I, 122; Fanfani, *De Iure Religiosorum,* p. 68.

[21] Canon 198, § 1.

[22] Thus Brys, "Explicatio Canonis 81,"—*Collationes Brugenses,* XXIX (1929), 145-146; and Lehmkuhl, *Theologia Moralis* (2 vols., 12. ed., Friburgi Brisgoviae, 1914), II, 478; Claeys Bouuaert-Simenon on the other hand (*Manuale,* I, 136), restrict the application of the "dispensari posse" to local ordinaries.

urgent case: Then ordinaries can dispense from the general laws of the Church provided recourse to Rome is difficult, and grave consequences would otherwise follow, and it is question of a case in which the Holy See generally grants the dispensation.

B. Commentary on Book II

11. Canon 94, §§ 1 and 2:

> **Sive per domicilium sive per quasi-domicilium suum quisque parochum et Ordinarium sortitur. Proprius vagi parochus vel Ordinarius est parochus vel Ordinarius loci in quo vagus actu commoratur.**

Since it is by religious profession and not by domicile or quasi-domicile that one is placed definitely under the jurisdiction of religious ordinaries, there can be no doubt that only the local ordinary is the ordinary referred to in this canon.[1]

---

[1] Concerning the question of religious and domicile, some very interesting questions can be raised. Oesterle ("De Domicilio Religiosorum,"—*CpRM*, V [1924], 167-178) has a long article on this subject in which he proposes and answers the following two questions: Do religious need a domicile? and: Can religious have a domicile? In general his answer is negative to both questions as far as exempt religious are concerned. He sums up his whole article in the following three propositions: "I. Religiosi qui jurisdictioni parochi subduntur, reguntur jure communi prout alii parochiani excepta ea materia, de qua specialiter providet ius (v. g. confessio sacramentalis, conciones habendae juxta can. 1338). II. Religiosi qui exempti sunt a jurisdictione parochi, sed subditi Ordinario loci, efformant in sua domo religiosa *paroeciam personalem* sui generis ad instar parochiae gentilitiae; juxta can. 94, § 3, *parochus loci* SECUNDARIE exercet jura parochialia in tales religiosos. III. Religiosi exempti tum a parocho tum ab Ordinario efformant in domo sua exempta *parochiam personalem exemptam,* in quam exercet Ordinarius loci suam jurisdictionem *tantum* in casibus a jure expressis (can. 615)."

12. Canons 114, 116, 117:

These canons deal with the canonical link by which a cleric is bound to his diocese and which is known as incardination, and with the act by which this link is severed and which is known as excardination. What has been said before in relation to canon 94 applies equally to these canons. Just as an exempt religious cannot have a domicile, so in like manner is he kept from being incardinated into a diocese. That by which a religious is bound to his institute is called religious profession and not incardination, except by analogy. At the most, as Maroto notes,[2] one may merely say that it is equivalent to incardination, even though the Code expressly states that by perpetual religious profession one is excardinated from his proper diocese[3] and that on

---

[2] *Institutiones,* I, 577: "Religiosorum clericorum adscriptio suae religioni nequit proprie incardinatio appellari, vel ad summum vocari posset incardinatio aequivalens aut improprie dicta, sicut recessus a religione posset ita aequivalens aut impropria excardinatio nuncupari. Sane illa religiosorum adscriptio et recessus a religione non sunt vere incardinatio nec excardinatio, quae tantum dioecesim aliquam respiciunt, unde in illa adscriptione et recessu non sunt servandae regulae et solemnitates incardinationis et excardinationis; sed tamen pro clericis religiosis aequivalet incardinationi sub pluribus respectibus; quatenus nempe per ipsam clerici religiosi vagi non sunt, sicuti nec clerici saeculares per incardinationem (c. 111, § 2); quatenus adscriptio religioni fert excardinationem non aliter fere ac incardinatio in dioecesi perficit excardinationem, et fieri nequit excardinatio quin subsequatur incardinatio." Of the same opinion are Coronata (*Institutiones,* I, 203) and Chelodi (*Ius de Personis,* p. 189). This is directly opposed, however, to the definition of terms made by Goyeneche (*Iuris Canonici Summa Principia,* p. 150): Incardinatio est "adscriptio perpetua et absoluta alicui dioecesi vel Religioni;" excardinatio est "discessio item perpetua et absoluta ab aliqua dioecesi vel Religioni." This opinion, although it seems to be a practical one, is against the terminology of the Code and certainly raises more questions than it solves, as can be seen by a perusal of the above-mentioned article of Oesterle (*CpRM,* V [1924], 167-178); therefore it seems better to hold the common opinion that exempt religious are according to the strict terminology neither incardinated nor excardinated.

[3] Canons 115 and 585.

leaving the religion one may again become incardinated in a diocese.[4]

13. Canon 126:

> **Omnes sacerdotes saeculares debent tertio saltem quoque anno spiritualibus exercitiis, per tempus a proprio Ordinario determinandum, in pia aliqua religiosave domo ab eodem designata vacare; neque ab eis quisquam eximatur, nisi in casu particulari, iusta de causa ac de expressa eiusdem Ordinarii licentia.**

At least every third year all diocesan priests must make a retreat for a certain length of time to be determined by the Ordinary in some pious or religious house designated by the bishop; no priest may be exempted from the retreat, except in a particular case for a just reason and with the explicit permission of the Ordinary.

Religious ordinaries are given no jurisdiction by reason of this canon as is evident from the text itself: "omnes sacerdotes saeculares." Ojetti,[5] Blat[6] and Berutti[7] all note expressly that the reason religious are not legislated for in this canon is that for religious there is a special canon which declares more accurately and more strictly the law in their regard.[8] In fact, the Code legislates that all diocesan priests shall make a retreat at least every three years while it prescribes an annual retreat for all religious.

Another evidence that this canon was not drawn up for religious is found in the letter of Pope Pius X who introduced the practice of having retreats into the discipline of the Church at Rome.[9] In this letter, written to Cardinal

---

[4] Canon 641, § 2.

[5] *Commentarium in Codicem Iuris Canonici* (4 vols., Romae: Apud Aedes Universitatis Gregorianae, 1927-1931), III, 89.

[6] *De Personis* (Romae: Apud Institutum Pontificium Internationale "Angelicum," 1921), p. 81.

[7] *Institutiones*, III, 243.

[8] Canon 595, § 1, n. 1.

[9] "*Experiendo,*" 27 dec. 1904—*Fontes*, n. 664.

Respighi, the Cardinal Vicar of Rome, the Holy Father decreed that all priests in Rome, *except religious,* should make a retreat at least every three years. The wording of the present canon is taken from that letter.

14. Canon 127:

Omnes clerici, praesertim vero presbyteri, speciali obligatione tenentur suo quisque Ordinario reverentiam et obedientiam exhibendi.

All clerics, but most especially priests, must show their own ordinary the proper reverence and obedience. With reference to religious the following norms should be considered. Nonexempt religious and, in the cases expressly mentioned in the Code, exempt religious are subject in obedience to the local ordinary because of his power of jurisdiction. All members in a religious community must obey the religious superiors of that community either by reason of their profession or, if they be novices or postulants, by reason of their physical admission into the community.[10] Moreover, all religious in an exempt clerical religion in addition owe obedience to their own major superiors because of their power of jurisdiction, for these latter are also ordinaries with authority in the external forum.[11]

The application of canon 127 to major superiors of exempt religions is wholly in agreement with the encyclical letter *"Neminem vestrum"* of Pope Pius IX, which is cited in the Gasparri edition of the Code as one of the sources for this canon. In part it reads as follows: "Vos etiam omnes ordinum affamur, Dilecti Filii Cleri cum Saecularis

---

[10] Cf. canon 561, § 2.

[11] Thus Vermeersch-Creusen, *Epitome,* I, 218; cf. also Blat, *De Personis,* p. 82; Mayer, *Benediktinisches Ordensrecht,* III, 225; Raus, *De Sacrae Obedientiae Virtute et Voto* (Lugduni, 1923), p. 30; Schaefer, *De Religiosis,* p. 661; Cocchi (*Commentarium,* II, 100), however, holds that this canon refers only to the diocesan clergy, and not to religious.

tum Regularis, . . . Propriis Antistibus, uti par est, subditi eisque obedientes ac memores vocationis et dignitatis vestrae, eam morum gravitate, vitae sanctitate exsequi ac tueri contendite."[12]

15. Canon 128:

> **Quoties et quandiu id, iudicio proprii Ordinarii, exigat Ecclesiae neccesitas, ac nisi legitimum impedimentum excuset, suscipiendum est clericis ac fideliter implendum munus quod ipsis fuerit ab Episcopo commissum.**

Any office assigned to clerics by the bishop must be accepted and faithfully discharged as often and as long as the proper ordinary judges that the needs of the Church demand it. Blat, arguing from the last words of the canon, "ab Episcopo commissum" and from the words "Ecclesiae necessitas," holds that the word *ordinary* here can refer only to the local ordinary.[13] But the words "ab Episcopo commissum" do not necessarily restrict the meaning of the words "iudicio proprii Ordinarii" of the first part of the canon. This very question was asked of the Sacred Congregation of the Council in 1890 and the answer was: ". . . quoad vero viros religiosos, quatenus extra claustra vivant de suorum superiorum temporanea licentia, rem agat [Episcopus] cum iisdem superioribus."[14] Moreover, by legitimate analogy[15] the phrase "ab Episcopo commissum" can be understood to refer also to any office imposed on a religious cleric by his own religious superior.[16]

---

[12] 2 febr. 1854, § 6—*Fontes*, n. 516.

[13] *De Personis*, p. 82; cf. also Cocchi, *Commentarium*, II, 100.

[14] S. C. C., *Calven.*, 28 mart. 1890—*Fontes*, n. 4278.

[15] Canon 20.

[16] Cf. Mayer, *Benediktinisches Ordensrecht*, III, 225; Schaefer, *De Religiosis*, p. 662; but especially Gerster a Zeil (*Ius Religiosorum* [Taurini: Marietti, 1935], p. 180) who paraphrases canons 127 and 128 as follows for religious: "Omnes . . . speciali obligatione tenentur suo quisque Ordinario (in religione clericali exempta Superiori maiori)

16. **Canon 136, § 3:**

Clerici minores qui propria auctoritate sine legitima causa habitum ecclesiasticum et tonsuram dimiserint, nec, ab Ordinario moniti, sese intra mensem emendaverint, ipso iure e statu clericali decidunt.

Clerics in minor orders, who of their own accord and without a legitimate reason fail to wear the ecclesiastical garb or the tonsure and do not obey within a month the admonition of their ordinary on this point, forfeit by that very fact the clerical state. This obligation is exchanged for religious into the obligation of wearing their own proper habit.[17] Moreover, since religious have their own legislation on this point, there is no reason why canon 136, § 3, also be applied to them. It must be remembered that this present canon provides for the punishment of those who without due permission lay aside the ecclesiastical garb. Therefore the canon must be strictly interpreted, i. e., to the exclusion of religious, according to the principle: "In poenis benignior est interpretatio facienda."[18] The punishment here mentioned is not to be applied to religious on the strength of this canon. Nevertheless it is clear to all that the laws for religious in this matter should be more strict than those for diocesan priests. But the infringement of such laws does not carry with it the incurring of any determined penalty. The application of some specific penalty is left to the prudent judgment of the religious superior.

---

reverentiam et obedientiam exhibendi. Quoties et quandiu id, iudicio proprii Ordinarii, exigat Ecclesiae necessitas, ac nisi legitimum impedimentum excuset, suscipiendum est clericis ac fideliter implendum munus quod ipsis fuerit . . . commissum." His omissions, as indicated by the dots, obviate in a very simple way any difficulties in applying the canons to religious and at the same time clearly express his mind concerning the applicability of these two canons to religious ordinaries.

[17] Canon 596; cf. also Vermeersch-Creusen, *Epitome,* I, 544; Berutti, *Institutiones,* III, 243; Segatori, *Lo Stato Religioso* (Torino, 1923), p. 181.

[18] Cf. canon 2219, § 1, and canon 19.

17. Canon 139, §§ 3 and 4:

§ 3. Sine licentia sui Ordinarii ne ineant [clerici] gestiones bonorum ad laicos pertinentium aut officia saecularia quae secumferant onus reddendarum rationum; procuratoris aut advocati munus ne exerceant, nisi in tribunali ecclesiastico, aut in civili quando agitur de causa propria aut suae ecclesiae; in laicali iudicio criminali, gravem personalem poenam prosequente, nullam partem habeant, ne testimonium quidem sine necessitate ferentes.

Without the permission of their ordinary, clerics should not undertake lay business affairs nor enter upon lay offices which involve the obligation of giving an account of one's affairs. Nor should clerics act as procurators or advocates, except in the ecclesiastical court, or also in the civil court when there is question of a general good for the Church or when they have been arraigned before such a court. Finally, clerics should not take part in lay criminal trials involving the possible infliction of a serious personal penalty; nor should they without necessity even act as witnesses in such cases. Religious ordinaries are implied in this paragraph on the strength of canon 592, by which religious are subject to the obligations which rest on all clerics as expressed in canons 124-142. Canon 592, it is true, says nothing about the superior (religious superior or local ordinary) who is to enforce these obligations; but naturally the religious superior is presumed in relation to exempt religious.[19] When there is question of a religious acting as an advocate, the prescription of canon 1657, § 3, must be followed, according

---

[19] Cf. Biederlack-Führich, *De Religiosis*, p. 230; Blat, *De Personis*, p. 100; Brunini, *The Clerical Obligations of Canons 139 and 142* (The Catholic University of America, Canon Law Studies, n. 103, Washington, D. C.: The Catholic University of America, 1937), p. 29; Coronata, *Institutiones*, I, 237; Maroto, "Annotationes,"—*CpRM*, I (1920), 98; Ojetti, *Commentarium*, III, 155; Papi, *Religious in Church Law* (New York, 1924), p. 122; Schaefer, *De Religiosis*, p. 665.

to which religious may be admitted provided that their constitutions do not forbid it, and provided that there is question of a case in which the good of their own religious institute is concerned. Even then they must have the permission of their superior.

§ 4. Senatorum aut oratorum legibus ferendis, quos *deputatos* vocant, munus ne sollicitent neve acceptent sine licentia Sanctae Sedis in locis ubi pontificia prohibitio intercesserit; idem ne attentent aliis in locis sine licentia tum sui Ordinarii, tum Ordinarii loci in quo electio facienda est.

This paragraph forbids clerics to present themselves as candidates for or to accept the office of senator or representative without the permission of their own ordinary and also of the ordinary of the place where the election is held. Moreover, in some countries, Italy for example, even the permission of the Holy See is required. In this country the permission of the ordinary is sufficient. Brunini sums up the legislation on this point clearly as follows: "A secular cleric, therefore, presenting himself to the electorate within his own diocese needs only the one permission of his own ordinary. A religious and those under the same discipline as religious must have a double permission. A secular cleric would also have need of a double permission if he desired to leave his own diocese and present himself to the electorate in another diocese."[20] A religious, therefore, in all cases must have two, no more no less, permissions, i.e., that of his own religious ordinary and that of the ordinary of the place where the election is held, whether or not this latter be the local ordinary of the place where his religious house is situated.

---

[20] *Op. cit.*, p. 60; cf. also Berutti, *Institutiones*, II, 244; Biederlack-Führich, *De Religiosis*, p. 230; Coronata, *Institutiones*, I, 237; Jansen, *Ordensrecht* (3. ed., Paderborn: Verlag Ferdinand Schöningh, 1931), p. 255.

18. Canon 141, § 1:

> **Saecularem militiam ne capessant voluntarii, nisi cum sui Ordinarii licentia, ut citius liberi evadant, id fecerint; neve intestinis bellis et ordinis publici perturbationibus opem quoquo modo ferant.**

Clerics are forbidden by this canon to volunteer for military service without the permission of their ordinary. Even then they should do so only in order that they may the sooner be finished with the service and thus become free to devote themselves to the sacred ministry. For his own subjects the ordinary from whom permission must be had will be the religious ordinary, as is clearly evidenced by the fact that after the last war the Holy See addressed a "Decretum de clericis e militia redeuntibus" to both local and religious ordinaries.[21]

19. Canon 143:

> **Clerici, licet beneficium aut officium residentiale non habeant, a sua tamen dioecesi per notabile tempus sine licentia saltem praesumpta Ordinarii proprii ne discedant.**

Clerics, even though they do not hold a benefice or office which demands residence, must not leave their diocese for any notable length of time without at least the presumed permission of their ordinary. From the very wording of this canon it can be seen that it was not drawn up for religious. It decrees "clerici . . . a sua . . . dioecesi . . . ne discedant" without at least the presumed permission of the ordinary. Canon 606 lays down the principles which should guide religious ordinaries in giving permission to their subjects to leave the religious enclosure. Naturally enough the restrictions in this regard are stringent. The patriarch of western monasticism, St. Benedict, considered this permanence of residence within the monastic enclosure so im-

---

[21] S. C. Consist., 25 oct. 1918—*AAS*, X (1918), 481-486; cf. also Berutti, *Institutiones*, II, 244; Blat, *De Personis*, p. 104.

portant to monasticism that he placed it first among the three vows which every newcomer to the monastery must make:

> Let him who is to be received make in the presence of all, in the oratory, a promise of stability, conversion of manners, and obedience, before God and His saints, so that, if he should ever act contrariwise, he may know that he is to be condemned by Him whom he mocks.[22]

20. Canon 149:

> **Electi, postulati, praesentati vel nominati a quibusvis personis ad ecclesiastica officia ne confirmentur, admittantur, instituantur a Superiore infra Romanum Pontificem, nisi antea fuerint a proprio Ordinario idonei reperti, etiam per examen, si id ius vel officii ratio postulet aut Ordinarius opportunum iudicaverit.**

"Candidates elected, postulated, presented or nominated by any persons for an ecclesiastical office shall not be confirmed, admitted or instituted by a superior below the Roman Pontiff, unless these persons have first been adjudged suitable by their respective Ordinary. The Ordinary thus has the right to subject them to an examination, if either the law or the nature of the office requires it, or the Ordinary judges it opportune."[23]

From canon 152 it is seen that the local ordinary has the right to provide for vacant offices in his diocese unless this right is proved to pertain to another. However, this right can be and is vindicated for religious ordinaries when there

---

[22] *The Holy Rule of St. Benedict* (Edited by the Benedictines of St. Meinrad's Abbey, St. Meinrad, Indiana: The Abbey Press, 1937), ch. 58; cf. also chapters 50 and 51; also the *Declarations and Constitutions of the Swiss-American Benedictine Congregation* (Conception Abbey, Conception, Mo.: Altar and Home Press, 1938), nn. 114 and 115.

[23] Woywod, *A Practical Commentary,* I, 61.

is question of appointment to offices within the monastery, e.g., the office of prior. In such a case the judgment concerning the fitness of the candidate rests entirely with the religious ordinary. Cocchi in his commentary on the Code says that with regard to offices in religion the judgment as to the worthiness of a candidate is made by the Roman Pontiff, if the provision or confirmation of the office pertains to him, or by the religious superior, or by the electors when the election needs no confirmation.[24] Ojetti, however, arguing against Blat, seems to deny that there are offices which pertain altogether to religious: "Non video quodnam sit discrimen inter ordinarium loci, ubi positum est officium, et illum, cui officium subiicitur conferendum. Nam ordinario loci subduntur per se omnes personae et res in suo territorio exsistentes et nonnisi ad summum per accidens fieri potest, ut aliqua res seu aliquod officium ecclesiasticum exemptum sit."[25] Ojetti's argument is based on a citation from Barbosa.[26] The citation, however, has no application to canon 149, for in this canon there is question of ecclesiastical offices, while Barbosa spoke only of ecclesiastical benefices. Even were it argued that Barbosa was speaking also of ecclesiastical offices in this text, yet it would seem, from other texts in his work, that he cannot be understood in the sense of Ojetti. For example, in *pars 3, alleg. 72, n. 125,* Barbosa wrote: "In beneficiis vero simplicibus, quorum collatio libere spectat ad inferiores, dicta Episcopi appro-

---

[24] *Commentarium,* II, 154; cf. also Ayrinhac, *General Legislation,* p. 319; Blat, *De Personis,* p. 116; Cappello, *Summa Iuris Canonici,* I, 353; Coronata, *Institutiones,* I, 251; Mayer, *Benediktinisches Ordensrecht,* II, 228-229; Schaefer, *De Religiosis,* p. 284.

[25] *Commentarium,* IV, 15, note 5.

[26] Ojetti, *Commentarium,* IV, 15, note 7: "... Cfr. Barbosa, De pot. episc., III, all. 60, n. 89; ... Hinc Barbosa, 1. c., n. 15: 'Abbas et alii, etiam iurisdictionem habentes ordinariam, non possunt instituere in beneficiis simplicibus praesentatum a patronis absque examine episcopi, ex hoc decreto et cap. 9 sess. 25 de ref., ... et aliter facta institutio est nulla ex eodem cap. 9 etiamsi praesentationes fiant coram abbatibus et aliis exemptionem a fundatione praetendentibus, si tantum illis exemptionibus innitantur. . .' "

batio non requiritur, sicut etiam in Canonicatibus Ecclesiarum collegiatarum, quorum collatio libere spectat ad Capitulum . . ."

This interpretation is confirmed by what Barbosa stated in other parts of his work. When treating of the devolution of the right to provide for vacant benefices he wrote: "In exemptis immediate Papae subiectis devolutio fit immediate ad Papam . . . Ratio est, quia ista devolutio . . . fit ad immediatum Superiorem, proximus autem Superior exemptorum est Papa . . ."[27] Again when he defined the different types of benefice he wrote: "Dicuntur autem regularia beneficia, de quibus in fundatione dictum fuit, ut per Religiosos regerentur . . . vel illa, quae per quadraginta annos consueta sunt regi per viros regulares."[28]

From these texts it is clear that according to the mind of Barbosa there were regular benefices wholly exempt from the local ordinary and ruled by the religious ordinary. More will be said about this question in the treatment of the canons on ecclesiastical benefices. Suffice it here to say that pre-Code legislation was very strict in limiting the powers of religious ordinaries whenever there was question of an office or benefice to which was attached the care of souls in a diocese; but it did not limit the jurisdiction and authority of religious ordinaries with respect to their own subjects.[29] Moreover, as Ojetti himself declares, it can

---

[27] *Op. cit.*, pars 3, alleg. 58, n. 13.

[28] *Op. cit.*, pars 3, alleg. 57, n. 168.

[29] Cf. Aichner, *Compendium Iuris Ecclesiastici* (10. ed., Brixiae, 1905), p. 30; Barbosa, *De Officio et Potestate Episcopi*, pars 3, alleg. 72, n. 125; Bouix, *De Iure Regularium* (3. ed., Parisiis, 1883), tom. II, 23-25; J. B. Sägmüller, *Lehrbuch des katholischen Kirchenrechts* (Freiburg im Breisgau, 1902), II, 241; Wernz, *Ius Decretalium*, t. III, pars 2, n. 683; for pontifical documents cf. Pius V, const. "*Romani Pontificis*", 21 iul. 1571—*Bullarum Diplomatum et Privilegiorum Sanctorum Romanorum Pontificum Taurinensis editio* (25 vols., Augustae Taurinorum, 1857-1872), VII, 930. Hereafter this work will be referred to as *Bullarium Taurinense*. Cf. also Benedictus XIV, const. "*Firmandis*", 6 nov. 1744, § 3—*Fontes*, n. 349; also Pius V, const. "*Ad exequendum*", 1 nov. 1567, §§ 4 and 5—*Bullarium Taurinense*, VII, 628-630.

happen that ecclesiastical offices may be exempted from the jurisdiction of the local ordinary. With regard to all offices in an exempt religion which pertain to the internal regimen of such a religion, the presumption according to canon 615 stands for their exemption from the jurisdiction of the local ordinary.

It is important to note here that the canons which concern ecclesiastical offices, namely, canons 145 to 195, as well as the later ones which concern benefices, namely, canons 1409 to 1488, must be interpreted with regard to religious in line with the demands of canons 499 to 515 and also in accord with the particular constitutions of the various religions.

21. Canon 157:

> **Officium vacans per renuntiationem vel per sententiam privationis nequit ab Ordinario, qui renuntiationem acceptavit aut sententiam tulit, valide conferri suis aut resignantis familiaribus, consanguineis vel affinibus usque ad secundum gradum inclusive.**

An office which becomes vacant either by resignation or by a sentence of privation cannot validly be conferred by the ordinary who accepted the resignation or declared the sentence: 1. on those of his own household or on those of the household of the recent incumbent of the office; 2. on his own relatives, whether they be such by blood or by marriage, to the second degree inclusive, or to the corresponding relatives of the recent incumbent. Coronata[30] and Blat[31] say that the restrictions contained in this canon apply to the religious ordinary as well as to the local ordinary. This opinion can be maintained for religions in which the religious are not forbidden to resign an office.[32]

---

30 *Institutiones*, I, 261.

31 *De Personis*, p. 124.

32 Cf. canon 184; also Cocchi, *Commentarium*, II, 205-206 and Mayer, *Ordensrecht*, II, 229.

Outside of this particular instance there would be no reason for these restrictions, because with regard to a religious who is "amovibilis ad nutum" there is no need of a sentence to deprive him of his office. If, therefore, the rule restricts the right of the religious to resign an office, neither of the two possible cases mentioned in the canon could be verified. On the other hand, the restrictions expressed in this canon would bind religious ordinaries in those religions in which the right of the religious subject to resign is not restricted, because this canon establishes the universal law, to which religious are also subject. The same reasons which advise such restrictions on the local ordinary have weight likewise with regard to a religious ordinary. These reasons are: 1. to obviate as much as possible the influence of natural affections and motives in choosing clerics for ecclesiastical offices and 2. to avoid any fraud.[33]

22. Canon 188, nn. 2, 7, 8:

This canon speaks of the various ways in which a man can tacitly resign his office. If there is nothing in the particular legislation of a religious institute contrary to this canon, its prescriptions will produce their effects for religious as well as for the members of the diocesan clergy.[34]

23. Canon 192, § 2:

Si agatur de officio inamovibili, Ordinarius nequit clericum eodem privare, nisi mediante processu ad normam iuris.

---

[33] Cf. Ferrari, *Summa Institutionum Canonicarum* (3. ed., 2 vols., Januae, 1877), II, 190, note 4; and Cocchi, *Commentarium,* II, 163; Claeys Bouuaert-Simenon, *Manuale,* I, 191.

[34] Cf. Wernz-Vidal, *Ius Canonicum,* III, 132, where he states that all religious can lose their offices in the same various ways as other clerics: "scl. per *mortem, renuntiationem, privationem, et depositionem* attentis praesertim singularum religionum statutis. Quibus modis apud regulares accedit *lapsus temporis* vel *revocatio ad nutum* legitimi Superioris facta." Cf. also Schaefer, *De Religiosis,* pp. 343-345.

The ordinary cannot, except by due process of law, deprive any cleric of his office if the cleric has been assigned to it as an irremovable incumbent. Religious are not included here because ordinarily they are not appointed as irremovable incumbents to any office. Offices in which the incumbency is intended to be permanent, such as the office of abbot, are not subject in any way to the control of the local ordinary, nor for that matter to the control of any religious ordinary. If any cause should arise to justify a deprivation of office in such a case, the act of deprivation would pertain solely to the Holy See. Coronata quite appositely remarks: "Pro officiis religiosorum ius speciale servandum est."[35]

24. Canon 192, § 3:

> **Si de amovibili [officio], privatio decerni ab Ordinario potest ex qualibet iusta causa, prudenti eius arbitrio, etiam citra delictum, naturali aequitate servata, sed certum procedendi modum sequi minime tenetur, salvo canonum praescripto circa paroecias amovibiles; privatio tamen effectum non habet, nisi postquam fuerit a Superiore intimata; et ab Ordinarii decreto datur recursus ad Sedem Apostolicam, sed in devolutivo tantum.**

In the case of an incumbent who is removable from office the deprivation may be decreed by the Ordinary for any just reason according to his prudent judgment, even though no canonical delict has been committed by the cleric. While the ordinary should observe natural equity, he is not bound to follow a certain form of procedure except in the removal of those pastors who fall under the prescriptions of canons 2157-2161. The deprivation of office has no effect until it has been communicated by the superior. Moreover, from the decree of the ordinary recourse to the Holy See is granted only "in devolutivo".

---

[35] *Institutiones*, I, 324.

This paragraph, with the exception of the phrase, "salvo canonum praescripto circa paroecias amovibiles", will certainly hold for religious as is evident from the constitution "*Firmandis*" of Benedict XIV[36] which is given in the footnote of the Gasparri edition of the Code as one of the sources for this paragraph. The phrase, however, "salvo canonum praescripto circa paroecias amovibiles" does not hold for religious because of canon 454, § 5, which decrees that all religious parish priests are "ratione personae, amovibiles ad nutum." With regard to the deprivation of other offices, the norms here laid down will apply to religious as well as to other clerics.

25. Canon 198, § 1:

Since this entire dissertation has for its purpose to show the application of this canon to the whole Code, very little need be said here. It will be recalled that in Chapter I of this thesis the extension of the application of the terms *ordinary* and *major superior* was declared. In Chapter II, also, the principles necessary for a correct understanding of the way in which this thesis has been developed are drawn from the present canon 198, § 1, and canon 631, § 2.

It is useful to point out here that the designation *ordinary* came into usage originally as a result of the fact that the holding of many offices in the Church carried with it a participation in the governing authority of the Church. This participation was called *ordinary jurisdiction*. In this original sense all those who enjoy ordinary jurisdiction can be called ordinaries. However, in the strict, canonical sense, as understood in the Code, those only are called ordinaries who have the right to exercise ordinary jurisdiction in both the external and internal forum.[37]

Wernz explains very well the reasons underlying the transference of quasi-episcopal authority to certain religious

[36] 6 nov. 1744, § 11—*Fontes*, n. 349.
[37] Cf. Wernz-Vidal, *Ius Canonicum*, II, 359.

superiors.[38] From the time that it became the usual thing for religious institutes of men to be exempt from the jurisdiction of the bishops and subject immediately to the Holy Father, there arose a moral necessity that the immediate religious superiors of these institutes themselves should have quasi-episcopal and ordinary jurisdiction, over and above the dominative power which all religious superiors have. It would be very inconvenient for the Roman Pontiff to rule these various communities immediately either personally or through individual delegates. Nevertheless every society must have authoritative and immediate leaders to guide and govern it in the various stages of its existence. With respect to exempt religious the authority of local ordinaries is excluded except in certain particular instances. Consequently the major religious superiors of these communities themselves were raised by the authority of the Roman Pontiff to the status of ordinaries.

That the power exercised by religious ordinaries is very similar to that which is exercised by bishops is clearly evidenced in various documents emanating from the Holy See. For example, the Constitution "*Romani Pontificis*" of Pius V has the following:

> Praelati regulares, ipsi per se ipsos idem omnino possunt in fratres et moniales . . . sibi subditos,

---

[38] *Ius Decretalium*, t. III, pars 2, n. 683: "Postquam religiones virorum saltem regulariter a iurisdictione *Episcoporum* fuerunt *exemptae* et *immediate Rom. Pontifici* subiectae, morali quadam necessitate factum est, ut Superiores regulares et prasertim capitula generalia *praeter potestatem dominativam* acquirerent *iurisdictionem quasiepiscopalem* vereque *ordinariam*. Nam quamprimum regulares a iurisdictione Episcoporum sunt exempti, immediate et per se a Rom. Pontifice vel eius delegatis convenienter gubernari non possunt. Omnis enim societas requirit pastores quosdam immediatos et ordinarios, qui *vi officii* regimen exercent; at Episcopi propter exemptionem sunt exclusi; ergo *intra ipsum ordinem religiosum* illi pastores ordinarii a R. Pontifice fuerunt instituendi." Cf. also *Dictionnaire de Droit Canonique* (fasc. I-XV, Paris, 1928-1939), s. v. "Abbés," I, 29-62, especially 42.

quod possunt episcopi in clericos et laicos sibi subjectos, tam quoad absolvendi et dispensandi hujusmodi, quam alias quascumque facultates, eadem auctoritate et tenore, etiam perpetuo concedimus, et indulgemus ac etiam declaramus.[39]

26. Canon 239, nn. 15 and 18:

Praeter alia privilegia quae in hoc Codice suis in titulis enumerantur, Cardinales omnes a sua promotione in Consistorio facultate gaudent:
15° Pontificalia cum throno et baldachino peragendi in omnibus ecclesiis extra Urbem, Ordinario praemonito, si ecclesia sit cathedralis.
18° Fruendi sacello ab Ordinarii visitatione exempto.

This canon enumerates the various privileges which all Cardinals enjoy. Number 15 states that a Cardinal can pontificate in any church outside Rome. If, however, the church is a cathedral, he should notify the ordinary beforehand. Number 18 gives him the right to have a chapel free from the visitation of the ordinary. The reference to the ordinary in both of these numbers is quite evidently to the local ordinary. Number 15 speaks of the ordinary of a cathedral church who can be only a local ordinary. The reference in number 18 is also clear if it be studied in conjunction with canons 344, § 1, and 1195, § 1, which impose upon the local ordinary the duty of canonical visitation relative to the private oratories in his diocese.[40] The private chapels of Cardinals are exempt from this visitation.

---

[39] 21 iul. 1571, § 3—*Bullarium Taurinense,* VII, 930; cf. also *Dictionnaire de Droit Canonique,* s. v. "Abbés," I, 42: "Tel est le pouvoir d'un évêque dans un diocèse. Celui d'un prélat régulier sur ses sujets est de même nature." Cf. also the decree of the Sacred Consistorial Congregation of October 25, 1918: *De clericis e militia redeuntibus—AAS,* X (1918), 481-486.

[40] Cf. Blat, *De Personis,* p. 229; Eichmann, *Lehrbuch des Kirchenrechts,* p. 151; Mothon, *Institutions Canoniques,* I, 146.

27. **Canon 239:**

22° Conferendi primam tonsuram et ordines minores, dummodo promovendus habeat dimissorias proprii Ordinarii litteras.

This number of canon 239 gives all cardinals the faculty to confer first tonsure and minor orders, provided the subject has the necessary dimissorial letters from his own proper ordinary. A religious ordinary, however, could grant such dimissorials to a cardinal only according to the prescriptions of canon 966, for canon 965 prescribes that the religious superior must send his subjects for ordination to the bishop of the diocese in which the religious house is situated. Canon 966 enumerates certain exceptions to this rule.

28. **Canon 247, § 4:**

Ad eandem [Congregationem Sancti Officii] pertinet non solum delatos sibi libros diligenter excutere, eos, si oportuerit, prohibere, et dispensationes concedere; sed etiam ex officio inquirere, qua opportuniore licebit via, quae in vulgus edantur scripta cuiuslibet generis damnanda, et in memoriam Ordinariorum reducere, quam religiose teneantur in perniciosa scripta animadvertere eaque Sanctae Sedi denuntiare, ad normam can. 1397.

This canon emphasizes the authority of the Holy Office with regard to the examination of books. Among other things it states that it is for this Sacred Congregation to devise means to counteract pernicious writings and also to bring home to the ordinaries their obligations in this matter. It is for the Holy Office alone to decide whether or not the communications they send out on this subject shall be sent to religious as well as to local ordinaries. Evidently the ordinaries principally referred to are local ordinaries, since they are, so to speak, the naturally responsible guardians of the christian faith and ecclesiastical discipline in their respective dioceses.[41]

29. Canon 274:

In dioecesibus vero suffraganeis Metropolita potest tantum:

5° Canonicam visitationem peragere, causa prius ab Apostolica Sede probata, si eam Suffraganeus neglexerit; tempore autem visitationis, potest praedicare, confessiones audire etiam absolvendo a casibus Episcopo reservatis, de vita et honestate clericorum inquirere, clericos infamia notatos Ordinariis ipsorum, ut eos puniant, denuntiare....

This canon speaks of the authority an archbishop enjoys when forced to conduct a canonical visitation in a diocese because of the proper ordinary's neglect or inability to do so. Among other things it is the duty of the archbishop to denounce to the ordinaries for punishment any clerics who are publicly branded with infamy. Blat,[42] arguing legitimately from canon 617, § 1, says that the ordinary referred to here may be either the local or the religious ordinary. Canon 617, § 1 states that, if abuses should occur in a church or house of an exempt religious and are not corrected by the religious superior after he has been notified of them, the local ordinary should report the matter to the Holy See. The archbishop, consequently, who is visiting a diocese in place of its proper bishop, would first warn the religious ordinary of any abuse. If it were not corrected or, with respect to canon 274, n. 5, if the cleric were not

---

[41] Cf. what has already been said above on this point in explanation of the words "nisi quis expresse excipiatur," *supra*, p. 5. Cf. also the notes on canon 1397, § 5, *infra*, p. 95.

[42] *De Personis*, p. 292: Metropolita "potest... d.) clericos infamia 'vel iuris vel facti' praesertim notatos ex publico proinde delicto, non iam punire, sed Ordinariis ipsorum sive loci, sive forsitan religiosis ad normam can. 616, 617 servandam, ut eos puniant, denuntiare efficaciter, unde si non punirentur, haberetur ex parte Ordinariorum abusus, quem consideravit canon in n. 4."

punished, the archbishop's duty would be to refer the matter to Rome.

30. Canon 696, § 2:

> **§ 1. Nemo, legitime adscriptus, ab associatione dimittatur, nisi iusta de causa ad normam statutorum.**
>
> **§ 2. Qui in casum inciderint, de quo in can. 693, § 1, expungantur, praemissa monitione, servatis propriis statutis et salvo iure recursus ad Ordinarium.**

No legitimately enrolled member of a society shall be dismissed from the association except for a good reason and according to the particular statutes of the society. Catholics who have fallen into one of the categories mentioned in canon 693, § 1 (that is, those who have joined a condemned society, who are notoriously under ecclesiastical censure, or who have in any other way become public sinners), shall after proper warning be expelled from the society by the competent official according to the particular statutes; the right of recourse, however, to the ordinary remains to them.[43]

When a religious ordinary has the Apostolic privilege to which canon 686, § 2, refers, namely, of erecting and of approving certain associations of the faithful, it seems that the local ordinary can not rightly act as arbiter in the cases of the sodality members, since he had nothing to do with the erection of the society itself. Or, to put the same thought in different words, since the Holy See by Apostolic privilege has reserved to the religious ordinaries the right of erecting and approving the associations here contemplated, it seems that *a fortiori* these same religious ordinaries are

---

[43] "Recursus ad Ordinarium est in devolutivo." Thus Goyeneche, *Iuris Canonici Summa Principia seu Breves Codicis Iuris Canonici Commentarii Scholis Accommodati, Partes II et III, Libri II* (Romae: Tip. Pol. "Cuore di Maria", 1938), p. 255.

also the ordinary superiors for the members of such societies on this point.

On the other hand, canon 696, § 3, gives to the local ordinary the power to expel members from *any* society, hence also from societies erected by religious ordinaries. In view of this consideration it seems that the recourse could be made also to him. Consequently, since the law does not precisely determine to which ordinary the recourse spoken of in this canon should be made, full liberty is left to the expelled member himself to choose whichever one he wishes.

If one should wish to determine more precisely those cases in which the local ordinary is peculiarly competent and those in which the recourse would more correctly be interposed with the religious ordinary, it would be necessary to make the following distinctions. The Code speaks of members who have been expelled for one of three reasons: 1.) because the member has joined a condemned society; 2.) because he is notoriously under ecclesiastical censure: excommunication, interdict, or suspension;[44] 3.) because he is a public sinner. If in any one of these cases the expelled member seeks recourse in order to have a decision made concerning some question of principle whose application would entail consequences in the whole diocese, then it would be more properly indicated to make this recourse to the local ordinary. But if the recourse is had merely to ask for reinstatement in the society, then it would be the logical procedure to have recourse to the religious ordinary.

Beil[45] and Mothon[46] in their commentaries seem to hold that this recourse is always to be made to the local ordinary, for they omit all mention of the religious ordinary. No argument, however, can be drawn from the silence of these authors relative to the religious ordinary. Neither author expressly excludes religious ordinaries; and neither of them gives any reason why the word *ordinary* in this

---

[44] Cf. canon 2255, § 1.

[45] *Das Kirchliche Vereinsrecht nach dem Codex Iuris Canonici* (Paderborn, 1932), p. 79.

[46] *Institutions Canoniques*, I, 904-905.

canon should be so restricted in meaning as to refer only to local ordinaries. In the absence, therefore, of any arguments to the contrary, and because of the reasons mentioned above, there seems to be no reasonable cause why the recourse mentioned in canon 696, § 2, could not be made to the religious ordinary.

C. Commentary on Book III

31. Canon 838:

> **Qui habent Missarum numerum de quibus sibi liceat libere disponere, possunt eas tribuere sacerdotibus sibi acceptis, dummodo probe sibi constet eos esse omni exceptione maiores vel testimonio proprii Ordinarii commendatos.**

One who has a number of Masses which he can freely dispose of can give them to any other priests he wishes, provided he is certain that such priests are fully trustworthy, or are recommended by their ordinaries. It is evident that for religious priests the recommendation of their own religious ordinary would be a sufficient testimonial regarding their reliability. Augustine,[1] however, disregards in this point religious ordinaries and thus comments on the canon: "Any priests may be freely chosen, provided they are absolutely reliable or recommended by the local Ordinary." Against this opinion there are the words "proprii Ordinarii" of the canon which according to a response of the Sacred Congregation of the Council[2] can refer only to the proper

---

[1] *A Commentary on the New Code of Canon Law* (8 vols., St. Louis, Mo.: Herder, Vol. I, 6. ed., 1931; Vol. II, 6. ed., 1936; Vol. III, 5. ed., 1938; Vol. IV, 3. ed., 1925; Vol. V, 5. ed., 1935; Vols. VI and VIII, 3. ed., 1931; Vol. VII, 3. ed., 1930), IV, 202.

[2] *AAS*, XIII (1921), 228-229: "Quibus verbis [canonis 838] apertissime conceditur facultas tradendi stipendia etiam extra dioecesim, si certae condiciones observentur, inter quas non reperitur permissio Ordinarii proprii transmittensis, sed sola commendatio Ordinarii sacerdotum quibus Missae celebrandae traduntur, si non sint bene noti transmittenti."

ordinary of him who is to receive the Mass stipends and not to the proper ordinary of the one who disposes of them. In view of this fact, if one were to distribute a number of stipends to an otherwise unknown exempt religious, it would be a sufficient testimonial if this religious priest had the commendation and approval of his own religious ordinary.[3]

32. **Canon 841, § 1:**

> **Omnes et singuli administratores causarum piarum aut quoquo modo ad Missarum onera implenda obligati, sive ecclesiastici sive laici, sub exitum cuiuslibet anni, Missarum onera quibus nondum fuerit satisfactum, suis Ordinariis tradant secundum modum ab his definiendum.**

All persons, cleric or lay, who have the obligation to say Masses or to see that they are said, must at the end of each year send to their ordinaries those Mass stipends which have not as yet been satisfied. It is only natural that such unsatisfied stipends, in the case of exempt religious, must be sent to the religious ordinary. Augustine[4] would again restrict the meaning of the word *ordinary* so as to include only the local ordinary, but he adduces no argument for his restrictive interpretation. Hence it may be supposed that he is not considering here religious and their obligations, but is speaking only of diocesan priests.

---

[3] Cf. Woywod, *A Practical Commentary,* I, 397; for documents concerning Mass stipends confer the following: Innocentius XII, const. *"Nuper,"* 23 dec. 1697—*Fontes,* n. 260; Benedictus XIV, *Institutiones Ecclesiasticae* (Romae, 1747), Instit. LXI; *idem., De Synodo Dioecesana* (3 vols., Romae, 1783), Vol. I, lib. V, cap. VIII; S. C. C., decr. *"Vigilanti,"* 25 maii 1893—*Fontes,* n. 4286; decr. *"Ut debita,"* 11 maii 1904—*Fontes,* n. 4317; 27 febr. 1905—*Fontes,* n. 4322. For an excellent treatise on this subject consult the *Dictionnaire de Théologie Catholique* (Vacant-Mangenot-Amann, XIV vols., Paris, 1903-1939), s. v. "Honoraires de Messes", VII, 769-791.

[4] *Commentary,* IV, 208.

The Council of Trent[5] decreed that the bishops, *abbots, and the generals of orders* should decide what was to be done whenever there was a superfluity of Mass stipends. The Code has extended this power to the major superiors of all exempt clerical religious. This is the opinion of Cappello,[6] Ayrinhac,[7] Schaefer,[8] Stadtmüller[9] and Woywod.[10] Other authors who were consulted do not express this opinion in precise words, but, if one judges from their inclusion of religious ordinaries under the term *ordinary* as it occurs in canon 843, § 2, one may easily presume that they hold a like opinion with regard to the present canon.

33. Canon 843, § 2:

> **Ordinarii tenentur obligatione singulis saltem annis huiusmodi libros [in quibus notantur Missarum receptarum numerum, intentionem, eleemosynam, celebrationem] sive per se ipsi sive per alios recognoscendi.**

All clerics charged with the care of churches or pious places in which stipends are customarily received are obliged to have a special book in which all Mass stipends received should be noted together with the intention for which they should be said, the offering that accompanied them, and finally, the date on which they were satisfied. The ordinaries are obliged to examine these books at least once a year, either personally or through a representative.

---

[5] Sess. XXV, *de ref.*, c. 4: "Ubi nimius est Missarum faciendarum numerus, statuant Episcopi, Abbates et Generales Ordinum, quod expedire judicaverint."

[6] *Tractatus Canonico-Moralis de Sacramentis* (3 vols. in 6, Taurinorum Augustae: Marietti, Vol. I, 3. ed., 1938; Vol. II, pars I, 3. ed., 1938; Vol. II, pars II, 1932; Vol. II, pars III, 1935; Vol. III, pars I, 4. ed., 1939; Vol. III, pars II, 4. ed., 1939), I, 712.

[7] *Legislation on the Sacraments in the New Code of Canon Law* (New York: Longmans, 1928), p. 151.

[8] *De Religiosis*, pp. 755-756.

[9] *Das neue Ordensrecht* (Dülmen, 1919), p. 111, note 3.

[10] *A Practical Commentary*, I, 401.

Since the duty of watching over the fulfillment of Mass obligations pertains in the different religious institutes to the superior,[11] the word *ordinary* in this canon will refer to religious ordinaries in all cases wherein Mass obligations of exempt clerical religions are concerned. For lay exempt and for all nonexempt religions the local ordinary must examine these books. This prescription by no means renders meaningless the aforementioned ruling with regard to religious. Arguing against Augustine[12] Woywod[13] reconciles the two canons as follows: "Canons 842 and 843 do not contradict each other. Canon 842 gives all religious superiors the right and duty to watch over the obligations arising from Mass stipends, and Canon 843 gives the Ordinary the right to inspect the Mass intention book at least once a year. That additional safeguard for the fulfillment of the obligations in non-exempt religious organizations cannot be called a contradiction." This is the common opinion.[14]

34. Canon 848:

> **§ 1. Ius et officium sacram communionem publice ad infirmos etiam non paroecianos extra ecclesiam deferendi, pertinet ad parochum intra suum territorium.**
>
> **§ 2. Ceteri sacerdotes id possunt in casu tantum necessitatis aut de licentia saltem praesumpta eiusdem parochi vel Ordinarii.**

---

[11] Canon 842.

[12] *Commentary*, IV, 211.

[13] *A Practical Commentary*, I, 402.

[14] Cf. Ayrinhac, *Legislation on the Sacraments*, p. 152; Cappello, *De Sacramentis*, I, 712 and 714; Mayer, *Ordensrecht*, II, 297; Schaefer, *De Religiosis*, p. 314 and pp. 755-756; Vermeersch-Creusen, *Epitome*, II, 73; Vromant, *De Bonis Ecclesiae Temporalibus ad usum utriusque cleri praesertim Missionariorum et religiosorum* (Louvain, 1927), p. 248; *idem*, "De Regimine Paroeciarum et Quasi-Paroeciarum Religiosis Sodalibus Concreditarum,"—*Ius Pontificium*, XIII (1933), 279.

The right and duty of publicly taking Holy Communion to the sick outside of the church and within the confines of his parish pertains to the pastor, even when the sick person is a stranger. No other priest can perform this pastoral duty unless it be a case of necessity or unless he has at least the presumed permission of the pastor or of the ordinary. From the context it is evident that the word *ordinary* refers exclusively to the local ordinary. Even canon 514, § 1, which gives religious superiors the right to administer Holy Viaticum and Extreme Unction to their own subjects does not derogate from the authority of the pastor and local ordinary as herein stated. The following doubt on just this point was proposed to the Pontifical Commission for the Interpretation of the Code on June 16, 1931.[15] "An Canon 514 § 1 ita intelligendus sit ut in religione clericali Superioribus jus et officium sit omnibus, de quibus in eodem canone, extra religiosam domum aegrotis Eucharisticum viaticum et Extremam Unctionem ministrandi. Resp. Affirmative, si agatur de religiosis professis vel novitiis, firmo tamen praescripto canonis 848; secus negative."

Therefore, if religious superiors wish to carry the Blessed Sacrament publicly to their religious or novices who are sick outside the religious house, they must have at least the presumed permission of the pastor or local ordinary unless it be a case of urgent necessity.[16]

35. **Canon 880, § 2:**

> **At graves ob causas Ordinarius potest etiam parocho aut poenitentiario confessarii munus interdicere, salvo recursu in devolutivo ad Sedem Apostolicam.**

---

[15] Cf. *AAS*, XXIII (1931), 353.

[16] Cf. Cappello, *De Sacramentis*, I, 289; Cosmas Sartori, *Enchiridion Canonicum* (Vicetiae: Ex Typographia Commerciali, 1938), p. 127; Vermeersch-Creusen, *Epitome*, II, 76; "Pont. Commissionis Codici J. C. Interpretando Praepositae Authentica Responsa,"—*Jus Pontificium*, XI (1931), 253.

Neither the local ordinary nor the religious superior should revoke or suspend the jurisdiction or permission to hear confessions except for a serious reason. However, if such a reason does exist, the ordinaries may do so, even with regard to pastors or canons confessors, although these two classes possess ordinary jurisdiction. This word *ordinary* in the second paragraph can also refer to religious ordinaries. Religious ordinaries, however, as Ayrinhac[17] well says, "can take away only the jurisdiction which they or their predecessors in office had granted. Withdrawal of jurisdiction by a religious superior would not prevent his subject from exercising validly, if not lawfully, the jurisdiction he has received from the local ordinary." The reason for this is found in canon 874, § 1, which says that the jurisdiction granted by local ordinaries is sufficient for the hearing of all confessions in a diocese, whether they be the confessions of lay persons or of religious, even exempt.[18] The same canon also declares that such jurisdiction should not be used by religious without at least the presumed permission of their own religious superiors.

Since canon 880, § 2, speaks only of pastors and canons confessors, it is evident that the religious ordinary could not suspend or revoke their jurisdiction to hear confessions although he could make the exercise of that jurisdiction illicit by forbidding them to hear confessions. He could, moreover, if he wished, remove religious pastors from their office, but even so, as long as they had jurisdiction from the bishop of the diocese, they could validly, although only illicitly, hear confessions.[19]

---

[17] *Legislation on the Sacraments*, p. 202.

[18] Cf. Woywod, *A Practical Commentary*, I, 424: "That the jurisdiction delegated by the bishop should extend even to the confessions of exempt religious, had been decreed by the Holy See a few years before the promulgation of the Code. The contrary privileges of some religious organizations, that their subjects could not be absolved except by a priest approved by the superior for the confessions of the religious, were revoked by that Decree." Cf. for this decree the Sacred Congregation of Religious, August 5, 1913—*AAS*, V (1913), 431.

[19] Augustine (*Commentary*, IV, 280) has the following: "... the

On the other hand, religious priests who have received jurisdiction only from a religious ordinary according to the prescriptions of canon 875, § 1, can not validly hear any confessions after the revocation or suspension of such jurisdiction by the religious ordinary.

36. Canon 883, § 1:

Sacerdotes omnes maritimum iter arripientes, dummodo vel a proprio Ordinario, vel ab Ordinario portus in quo navim conscendunt, vel etiam ab Ordinario cuiusvis portus interiecti per quem in itinere transeunt, facultatem rite acceperint confessiones audiendi, possunt, toto itinere, quorumlibet fidelium secum navigantium confessiones in navi excipere, quamvis navis in itinere transeat vel etiam aliquandiu consistat variis in locis diversorum Ordinariorum iurisdictioni subiectis.

For the duration of the trip all priests on an ocean voyage can hear the confessions of those who travel with them, provided they have jurisdiction either from their own ordinary, or from the ordinary of the port from which, or of the port to which, they are sailing. The word *ordinary* in this canon can never refer to religious ordinaries. Since the Code says "a proprio Ordinario", there was at first a very prudent doubt as to whether the jurisdiction granted by a religious ordinary was sufficient to hear confessions at sea.[20] The Pontifical Commission for the Interpretation

---

local ordinary may also forbid the pastor or canon penitentiary to exercise the office of confessor..." This is in itself true; but the canon gives the same power also to religious ordinaries. Cf. also canon 631, § 2. This is the opinion of Ayrinhac, as above cited; Cappello, *De Sacramentis*, II, pars I, 315; and Schaefer, *De Religiosis*, p. 829; cf. also S. C. Ep. et Reg., *Ordinis Praedicatorum*, 2 mart. 1866—*Fontes*, n. 1996.

[20] Cf. Bouscaren, *Canon Law Digest* (2 vols. and 2 supplements, Milwaukee: Bruce, 1934-1941), II, 90; Schaefer, *De Religiosis*, p. 832; Petrus Voltas, "Consultationes,"—*CpRM*, II (1921), 373; A. Vermeersch, "*Quid Ordinarius* in can. 883 C. I. C.,"—*Periodica*, XXII

of the Code dispelled all doubts, however, by its decision of July 30, 1934. It excluded the authority of religious ordinaries in this matter.[21]

37. Canon 899, § 3:

> **Ipso iure a casibus, quos quoquo modo sibi Ordinarii reservaverint, absolvere possunt tum parochi, aliive qui parochorum nomine in iure censentur, toto tempore ad praeceptum paschale adimplendum utili, tum singuli missionarii quo tempore missiones ad populum haberi contingat.**

Pastors during the entire paschal time and missionaries while they are conducting a mission have *ipso iure* the faculty of absolving from all cases which the ordinary has in any way reserved to himself. Although strictly taken the word *ordinary* here includes religious ordinaries, yet, because of the principle stated in canon 519, which enables any confessor, if he be approved by the local ordinary for the hearing of confessions, to absolve a religious even from such sins and censures as are reserved in his religious institute, such an inclusion of religious ordinaries under the word *ordinary* will have little if any practical consequence.

The question, however, may be asked: What faculties with regard to cases which the major superior of an exempt clerical religion has reserved to himself has a priest who has received his faculties to preach and hear confessions only from this same religious ordinary[22] and not also from the local ordinary? In that case it must be answered that such a priest has those faculties and only those faculties which the religious ordinary has granted him. If, therefore, he

---

(1933), 32*-34*; *idem*, "Pontificia Commissio Interpretando Codici,"—*Periodica*, XXIII (1934), 147; Albertus Canestri, "De Confessione Navigantium,"—*Apollinaris*, VIII (1935), 60-61; Maroto, "De Confessione Navigantium,"—*CpRM*, XV (1934), 356-358; "Quaesiti Minori,"—*Il Monitore Ecclesiastico*, XXXIII (1921), 285.

[21] Cf. *AAS*, XXVI (1934), 494.

[22] Cf. canons 875, § 1 and 1338, § 1.

has not received the special faculty to absolve from the reserved cases concerning which there is question here, he cannot take it upon himself to exercise that faculty.

38. Canon 968, § 1:

> **Sacram ordinationem valide recipit solus vir baptizatus; licite autem, qui ad normam sacrorum canonum debitis qualitatibus, iudicio proprii Ordinarii, praeditus sit, neque ulla detineatur irregularitate aliove impedimento.**

Baptized men alone can validly be ordained; for licit ordination a man must, moreover, in the judgment of his own ordinary, be gifted with the proper canonical qualifications and must be free from all irregularities or impediments. The word *ordinary* here undoubtedly refers also to religious ordinaries.[23] Nevertheless the observation of Ayrinhac on this canon is correct. He writes: "This canon directly concerns the secular clergy, not religious, except implicitly and by way of general direction.[24]

39. Canon 972, § 1:

> **Curandum ut ad sacros ordines adspirantes inde a teneris annis in Seminario recipiantur; sed omnes ibidem commorari tenentur saltem per integrum sacrae theologiae curriculum, nisi Ordinarius in casibus peculiaribus, gravi de causa, onerata eius conscientia, dispensaverit.**

This canon lays upon all ordinaries the obligation of providing that all candidates for the priesthood should live in the seminary during the entire course of Sacred Theology. But it also gives the ordinary the power of dispensing from this rule in particular cases and for grave reasons; for such dispensations he is held responsible in conscience. Religious

---

[23] Cf. Gerster a Zeil, *Ius Religiosorum*, pp. 298-299; Schaefer, *De Religiosis*, p. 833, note 66.

[24] *Legislation on the Sacraments*, p. 326.

students for the priesthood are also bound by this canon. But over and above this, they are also subject to the more exacting regulations of canon 587, § 4, and the special Instruction of the Sacred Congregation for Religious.[25] However, in virtue of canon 972, § 1, whose influence is evident in the Instruction of the Sacred Congregation,[26] religious ordinaries can grant a dispensation from these conditions.[27]

40. Canon 984, 3°:

Sunt irregulares ex defectu: Qui epileptici vel amentes vel a daemone possessi sunt vel fuerunt; quod si post receptos ordines tales evaserint et iam liberos esse certo constet, Ordinarius potest suis subditis receptorum ordinum exercitium rursus permittere.

This canon declares that all those who suffer, or who have suffered, from epilepsy, insanity, or diabolical possession are canonically irregular for the reception or exercise of orders. But if a person, after he has received orders, suffers from one of these causes and then fully recovers, the ordinary can permit him once again to exercise the orders received. If the one who has suffered these attacks is a religious, it will be the religious ordinary who will judge as to whether or not the person is to exercise his orders.[28]

---

[25] "De Formatione clericali et religiosa alumnorum,"—*AAS*, XXIV (1932), 74 ff., especially n. 9.

[26] The canon reads: "nisi Ordinarius in casibus peculiaribus, gravi de causa, onerata eius conscientia, dispensaverit," while the Instruction is as follows: ". . . ideo non absque iusta et gravi causa, de qua re Superiorum conscientia graviter onerata manet, eosdem itinera suscipere liceat, sed in domibus ad studia destinatis constanter permaneant; ibique, in exercitia pietatis ac scientiae, usque ad completum studiorum curriculum, incumbant assidue."

[27] Cf. Brys, "Explicatio canonis 81,"—*Collationes Brugenses*, XXIX (1929), 145, note 1; Reilly, *The General Norms of Dispensation*, p. 66, note 45.

[28] Cf. Augustine, *Commentary*, IV, 482-483; Cappello, *De Sacramentis*, II, pars III, 455; and Stadtmüller, *Das neue Ordensrecht*, p. 167, note 2.

41. Canon 987: Sunt simpliciter impediti:

6° Neophyti, donec, iudicio Ordinarii, sufficienter probati fuerint;

7° Qui infamia facti laborant, dum ipsa, iudicio Ordinarii, perdurat.

These two numbers of canon 987 declare that neophytes, until they are sufficiently proved, and men who have lost their good name, until it has been recovered, are impeded from the reception or exercise of orders. The judgment as to whether a man is sufficiently grounded in the faith or as to the fact that he has recovered his good name rests with the ordinary. That by the term *ordinary* in this canon is meant, for his own subjects, the religious ordinary is clear if we consider that for religious it is the religious ordinary who has the final responsibility as to the worthiness of his subjects when they are presented for orders. Canon 995, § 2, explicitly declares that an ordaining bishop needs no other testimonial letters once he has obtained the dimissorials from the legitimate religious superior. Cappello[29] in commenting on this canon, says correctly: "Hinc patet litteras dimissorias pro ordinatione religiosorum cumulari cum litteris testimonialibus: idque ex ipso iuris praescripto." The same can also be gathered from a decree of the Sacred Congregation of Religious issued on Jan. 1, 1911, which reads as follows: "Superiores Generales aut Provinciales etiam locales, iuxta uniuscuiusque Instituti morem, per se vel delegatum sodalem . . . de vita, moribus et conversatione alumnorum, perdurante militari servitio, inquirere omnino teneantur, opera praecipue sacerdotis vel sacerdotum, de quibus supra, per secretas epistolas, si opus sit, ut certiores fiant, an ii rectam fidei et morum viam servaverint, cautelas supra praescriptas observaverint et divinae vocationi se fideles praebuerint, graviter onerata eorum conscientia."[30]

---

[29] *De Sacramentis*, II, pars III, 297.

[30] *Fontes*, n. 4408.

With regard to canon 987, n. 6, Augustine,[31] Ayrinhac[32] and Wernz-Vidal[33] hold that the judgment concerning neophytes should rest with the local ordinary. Undoubtedly the local ordinary will be the one who will have to judge in the majority of cases. But it can be conceived that the religious ordinary would sometimes, even if rarely, be concerned. For example, let it be supposed that a neophyte after one year in the Church enters a religious order. The year of novitiate passes; likewise the two years of philosophy. Theology is begun and the candidate is ready for tonsure and minor orders. Should there exist any doubt as to whether this man is sufficiently grounded in the faith or not, then certainly the judgment concerning him would rest with the religious ordinary. If one considers the mutability of disposition existing in all men, one can readily imagine that even after four years there might sometimes be a seriour doubt with regard to a convert's constancy of mind and purpose in his recent conversion to the faith.

With reference to canon 987, n. 7, there seems to be no reason for doubting that, for his own subjects, it will be the religious ordinary who will decide whether the candidate has recovered his good name.[34] If, however, the religious has lost his good name not only within, but also outside the religious institute, then it will be for the local ordinary also to judge about the matter according to the principles enunciated in canons 973, § 3 and 997, § 2.

42. Canon 990:

> **§ 1. Licet Ordinariis per se vel per alium suos subditos dispensare ab irregularitatibus omnibus ex delicto occulto provenientibus, ea excepta de qua in can. 985, n. 4 aliave deducta ad forum iudiciale.**

---

[31] *Commentary,* IV, 500.

[32] *Legislation on the Sacraments,* p. 374.

[33] *Ius Canonicum,* IV, pars 1, 351.

[34] Cf. Blat, *De Sacramentis* (Romae, 1924), p. 443.

§ 2. Eadem facultas competit cuilibet confessario in casibus occultis urgentioribus in quibus Ordinarius adiri nequeat et periculum immineat gravis damni vel infamiae, sed ad hoc dumtaxat ut poenitens ordines iam susceptos exercere licite valeat.

This canon grants to all ordinaries, therefore also to major superiors of exempt clerical religions, the power to dispense their own proper subjects from all irregularities which are caused by any occult crime mentioned in canon 985, except the irregularity arising from voluntary homicide or from abortion. Authors are unanimous on this point.[35] Moreover, as Ayrinhac[36] rightly observes, it not infrequently happens that religious ordinaries, by virtue of special privileges received, may dispense from *all* irregularities without exception, at least in the internal forum.[37]

43. Canon 994, § 2:

Si loci Ordinarius neque per se neque per alios promovendum satis noverit, ut testari possit eum, tempore quo in suo territorio moratus est, nullum

---

[35] Cf. Augustine, *Commentary,* IV, 504; Brys, "De Potestate Episcoporum Dispensandi in Legibus Ecclesiae Generalibus,"—*Collationes Brugenses,* XXIX (1929), 145, note 1; Claeys Bouuaert-Simenon, *Manuale,* I, 134; Cappello, *De Sacramentis,* II, pars III, 483; Fanfani, *De Iure Religiosorum,* p. 69; John J. Hickey, *Irregularities and Simple Impediments in the New Code of Canon Law* (The Catholic University of America, Canon Law Studies, n. 7, Washington, D. C.: The Catholic University of America, 1920), p. 87; Michiels, *Normae Generales,* II, 480; Schaefer, *De Religiosis,* p. 236; Vermeersch-Creusen, *Epitome,* I, 168; Wernz-Vidal, *Ius Canonicum,* I, 471; Woywod, *A Practical Commentary,* I, 544; Beste, *Introductio in Codicem,* p. 536.

[36] *Legislation on the Sacraments,* p. 379.

[37] Cf. F. Lucius Ferraris, *Prompta Bibliotheca, Canonica, Juridica, Moralis, Theologica necnon Ascetica, Polemica, Rubricistica, Historica* (ed. Migne, 8 vols., Parisiis, 1860-1863), s. v. "Regularis Praelatus," nn. 14, 16, 27; "Absolvere," nn. 29-40; "Abbas"; cf. also Pius V, const. "*Dum ad congreg. Cassinensem,*" 13 iun. 1571—*Bullarium Taurinense,* VII, 919-921.

canonicum impedimentum contraxisse, aut si promovendus per tot dioeceses vagatus sit ut impossibile vel nimis difficile evadat omnes litteras testimoniales exquirere, provideat Ordinarius saltem per iuramentum suppletorium a promovendo praestandum.

Canon 993, n. 4, prescribes that every candidate for the priesthood, be he for the diocesan or the religious clergy, must provide testimonial letters from each local ordinary in whose territory the candidate has remained long enough, morally considered, to contract a canonical impediment. Canon 994, § 1, defines more precisely the length of time which regularly is considered long enough to contract such an impediment. Paragraph two of this canon says that if the candidate has travelled around so extensively that it would be very difficult to obtain all such testimonials, then the ordinary should make up for the lack of these letters by demanding at least a supplementary oath from the candidate. Although Cappello[38] at first states clearly that this obligation of demanding an additional oath rests with the *proper* ordinary of him who is to be ordained (therefore, it would seem, with the religious ordinary for his own subjects), yet in the next line he excludes religious ordinaries with the following short but very clear sentence: "Iuramentum suppletorium praestandum est coram Ordinario loci eiusve delegato." However, it does not seem contrary either to the spirit or to the letter of the Code to hold that, for his own subjects, the ordinary referred to here will be the religious ordinary. This opinion is based on the fact that major superiors of exempt clerical religions are ordinaries for their own subjects, and secondly on the fact that the Code here uses the word *ordinary* without any modification. Augustine[39] states the whole situation very well as follows: "But if a religious has to undergo *military service* (as in France and Italy) the religious must obtain *litterae testi-*

[38] *De Sacramentis,* II, pars III, 505.

[39] *Commentary,* IV, 519.

moniales from each and every Ordinary in whose diocese the candidate spent at least three months. However, in the case mentioned in can. 994, § 2, namely, when it is impossible or difficult to obtain all these testimonials, the religious superior—for he is the Ordinary of the *ordinandus*—may demand a supplementary oath from the candidate as to his freedom from canonical impediments."

It is to be noted here that Augustine says the religious ordinary *may* demand such an oath. Since the canon says "provideat" and "saltem", there is a real obligation for the ordinary to demand the oath if he has not the testimonials and provided that the ordaining prelate himself does not demand it.

44. Canons 998 and 1000:

> **Canon 998, § 1. Nomina promovendorum ad singulos sacros ordines, exceptis religiosis a votis perpetuis sive sollemnibus, sive simplicibus, publice denuntientur in paroeciali cuiusque candidati ecclesia; sed Ordinarius pro sua prudentia potest tum ab hac publicatione dispensare ex iusta causa, tum praecipere ut in aliis ecclesiis peragatur, tum publicationi substituere publicam ad valvas ecclesiae affixionem per aliquot dies, in quibus unus saltem dies festus comprehendatur.**
> **§ 3. Si sex intra menses candidatus promotus non fuerit, repetatur publicatio, nisi aliud Ordinario videatur.**
>
> **Canon 1000, § 1. Parocho qui publicationem peragit, et etiam alii, si id expedire videatur, Ordinarius committat ut de ordinandorum moribus et vita a fide dignis diligenter exquirat, et litteras testimoniales, ipsam investigationem et publicationem referentes, ad Curiam transmittat.**
>
> **§ 2. Idem Ordinarius alias percontationes etiam privatas, si id necessarium aut opportunum iudicaverit, facere ne omittat.**

The names of all those who are to be promoted to any major order, with the exception of those religious who have perpetual vows, must be publicly announced in the respective parish churches of the candidates, unless the ordinary for a just cause sees fit to dispense from this obligation. The ordinary here referred to can never be a religious ordinary, as is evident from the fact that the names of a religious ordinary's subjects need never be thus announced.[40]

45. Canon 999:

> **Omnes fideles obligatione tenentur impedimenta ad sacros ordines, si qua norint, Ordinario vel parocho ante sacram ordinationem revelandi.**

This canon obliges all the faithful to reveal to the ordinary or parish priest any impediment to sacred orders, which they may be aware of, on the part of any of the candidates. No special commentary is needed here. Quite evidently a man would fulfill the obligation of this canon if he would reveal the impediment of a religious candidate for orders to the religious ordinary.

46. Canon 1001:

> **§ 1. Qui ad primam tonsuram et ordines minores promovendi sunt, spiritualibus exercitiis per tres saltem integros dies; qui vero ad ordines sacros, saltem per sex integros dies vacent; sed si qui, intra semestre, ad plures ordines maiores promovendi sint, Ordinarius potest exercitiorum tempus pro ordinatione ad diaconatum reducere, non tamen infra tres integros dies.**

---

[40] Cf. Schaefer, *De Religiosis*, p. 839. Because of the reason given in the text it is hard to see why the following two authors enumerate this canon as referring to all ordinaries, even those who are not local ordinaries: Brys, "De Potestate Episcoporum Dispensandi,"—*Collationes Brugenses*, XXIX (1929), 145; and Stadtmüller, *Das neue Ordensrecht*, p. 172.

§ 2. Si, expletis exercitiis, sacra ordinatio qualibet de causa ultra semestre differatur, exercitia iterentur; secus iudicet Ordinarius utrum iteranda sint, necne.

Before receiving first tonsure or the minor orders one must make a retreat for at least three full days. Those, however, who are to receive one of the major orders, must make a retreat of at least six full days. If one receives two or all three major orders within one semester, the ordinary may shorten somewhat the retreat which immediately preceeds the reception of the diaconate; but even then it must be always at least three full days. If the ordination is postponed for longer than six months after the candidate has duly made the retreat according to the rule of this canon, then the retreat must be repeated; otherwise the ordinary is to decide whether it should be repeated or not. In both of these cases the ordinary for exempt clerical religious will be either the ordaining ordinary or the religious ordinary. Ordinarily, of course, it will be the religious ordinary.[41]

47. Canon 1010, § 2:

Singulis ordinatis detur authenticum ordinationis receptae testimonium; qui, si ab Episcopo extraneo cum litteris dimissoriis promoti fuerint, illud proprio Ordinario exhibeant pro ordinationis adnotatione in speciali libro in archivo servando.

There must be given to each cleric who has been ordained an authentic document which attests his ordination. He who has been ordained with the intervention of dimissorial letters must show the document which attests this fact to his own proper ordinary for notation in the archives. Evidently the proper ordinary for exempt religious is the re-

[41] Cf. Ayrinhac, *Legislation on the Sacraments*, p. 391; Cappello, *De Sacramentis*, II, pars III, 515; Papi, *Religious in Church Law*, p. 214; Stadtmüller, *Das neue Ordensrecht*, p. 173; Vermeersch-Creusen, *Epitome*, II, 184.

ligious ordinary.[42] The argument of Pejška,[43] who says that this canon does not bind religious because the diocesan bishop is not their proper ordinary, does not touch the point in question. The proper ordinary of an exempt religious is his own major superior who, according to the rule of canon 1010, § 2, must be shown the certificate of the ordination of his subjects in order that he may note the fact in the archives of the religious institute.

48. Canon 1151:

§ 1. Nemo, potestate exorcizandi praeditus, exorcismos in obsessos proferre legitime potest, nisi ab Ordinario peculiarem et expressam licentiam obtinuerit.

§ 2. Haec licentia ab Ordinario concedatur tantummodo sacerdoti pietate, prudentia ac vitae integritate praedito; qui ad exorcismos ne procedat, nisi postquam diligenti prudentique investigatione compererit exorcizandum esse revera a daemone obsessum.

No one who has the faculty of exorcizing persons possessed by the devil can legitimately use such a faculty without first having obtained the special and express permission of his ordinary. This latter shall grant such permission only to priests whom he knows to be men of piety, prudence and integrity. Since the Code uses the word *ordinary* here without any modification, it seems tenable that the religious ordinary could give the requisite permission for any case in which one of his subjects should need to be exorcized. This is the express opinion of Vermeersch-

---

[42] Thus Cappello, *Summa Iuris Canonici,* II, 583; and Stadtmüller, *Das neue Ordensrecht,* p. 174.

[43] *Ius Canonicum Religiosorum* (3. ed., Friburgi Brisgoviae: Herder, 1927), p. 311: "Religiosi exempti, qui secundum can. 966 ab alio quam dioecesano Episcopo ordinati sunt, huic legi non sunt obnoxii, quia Episcopus dioecesanus non est eorum Ordinarius proprius."

Creusen[44] and of Augustine.[45] Wernz-Vidal, however, hold the opposite opinion.[46] The argument of these authors is based on two constitutions of Pope Benedict XIV, on a response of the Holy Office and on the decrees of various provincial councils from the year 1699 to 1865, as given in the *Collectio Lacensis.* Each one of these allegations should be considered separately.

a.) The Constitution *Sollicitudini,* October 1, 1745, § 43, of Pope Benedict XIV:[47] The phrase that is pertinent to the presently contemplated canon is: "...eligatur ab Ordinario sacerdos..." This text cannot be adduced in itself to prove that religious ordinaries have not the same power with regard to their own subjects, for the Pontiff is writing to bishops and hence does not directly consider the question in so far as it refers to exempt religious.

b.) The Constitution *Magno cum,* June 2, 1751, § 34, of Pope Benedict XIV:[48]

> In eo, qui ad Nos factus est, recursu, alterius etiam inconvenientis mentio fit, quod scilicet, sine licentia vestra, Regulares exorcizent; de hoc tamen nihil dicitur utrum per Vos, aut in Synodis vestris, aut in vestris Edictis decretum fuerit, ne ullus Sacerdos, vel Saecularis, vel Regularis exorcizare audeat, sive in sua, sive in aliena Ecclesia, sive intra, sive extra Coenobium, quin prius a vobis approbatus sit, atque ita, quin ante licentiam a vobis obtinuerit. Hoc illud est, quod praestari debet, quodque ab Episcopis praestari solet, quemadmo-

---

44 *Epitome,* II, 323.

45 *Commentary,* IV, 569.

46 *Ius Canonicum,* IV, pars 1, 403: "Ex disciplina vero vigente ad huiusmodi exorcismum nomine Ecclesiae et in forma publica nemo ex clero sive saeculari sive regulari procedere potest, nisi sit sacerdos et insuper ab Ordinario loci in singulis casibus peculiarem et expressam obtineat licentiam." In a footnote are given the sources for this opinion.

47 *Fontes,* n. 362.

48 *Fontes,* n. 413.

> dum apud Clericatum, *de Sacramento Ordinis,* decis. 19, num. 42, ubi Episcopales Synodos affert, videre licet.

Judging from the text of this papal constitution one is led to the conclusion that unless the bishop in a synodal or other decree had forbidden it, the religious ordinary was not forbidden to give such permission.

c.) The response of the Holy Office, July 5, 1710:[49]

> Tertio requiritur, ut Exorcizatio solemnis fiat ab habente potestatem, quae non omnibus conceditur, sed tantum aliquibus, secundum prudentiam Episcoporum, habentibus ordinem Ecclesiasticum Exorcistatus ... Unde nemo potest exorcizare sine facultate Ordinarii, etiamsi sit Regularis, ut decrevit Sacra Congregat. Episcop. et Regul. in Florentina 22 Februarii 1625, et expresse statuit Sacr. Congregat. S. Officii die 5 Iul. 1710 per litteram Encyclicam directam omnibus Archiepiscopis aliisque Ordinariis Italiae et Insularum adiacentium, tenoris ut sequitur: "... che in avvenire non permetta, che alcun Sacerdote tanto Secolare quanto Regolare, sia ammesso all'esercizio de Ezorcista, senza che prima le costi della di lui pietà, integrità di vita e prudenza, e senza che abbia tutte le qualità ricercate per tale amministrazione dal Rituale Romano ...

This letter from the Holy Office was directed to the ordinaries of Italy. Although it is construed in general terms, yet it can, without any forced interpretation be understood as not referring to the possible exorcism of a regular in his own religious house. Moreover, it may be concluded that

[49] The following excerpted explanation and also the cited text of the response of the Holy Office are borrowed from Ferraris, *Bibliotheca,* s. v. "Exorcizare, Exorcista," nn. 8, 9. The entire text of the response could not be found in the *Collectanea* of Bizzarri, nor in the *Collectanea S. C. de Prop. Fide* nor in the *Fontes Iuris Canonici.*

this is the way the above cited encyclical of the Holy Office was understood from the fact that Ferraris in the same article, n. 20, stated that regulars could not exorcize a possessed person, even in their own proper churches and houses, *if* the bishops forbade it: "Regularibus non licet, contradicente Episcopo, exorcizare, etiam in propriis Ecclesiis et Coenobiis." Therefore, if the local ordinary did not forbid it, regulars could perform the exorcism with the permission of their own religious ordinary.

d.) The text of the various provincial councils cited by Wernz-Vidal[50] can also be understood in this same way. After studying the various sources, one arrives at the conclusion that, since it is a matter which often of its very nature becomes a public event, and since it is a matter that pertains so directly to faith and divine worship, all exorcisms in a diocese must be under at least the vigilance of the local ordinary. Therefore, if he were to make a ruling that not even exempt religious in their own churches or communities could exercise the faculty of exorcizing a possessed person, such a ruling would certainly be valid and binding. Wherever he has not made such a law, the religious ordinary also, in virtue of canon 1151, can give his subjects the permission to use this power of exorcism for the benefit of his own subjects.

49. Canon 1157:

> **Non obstante quolibet privilegio, nemo potest locum sacrum consecrare vel benedicere sine Ordinarii consensu.**

No one, no matter how he may be privileged, can consecrate or bless a place set aside for divine worship without

[50] *Constitutiones Synodi prov. Neapolitanae a. 1699*, tit. III, cap. VIII—*Acta et Decreta Sacrorum Conciliorum Recentiorum, Collectio Lacensis* (7 vols., Friburgi Brisgoviae, 1870-1892), I, 197; *Decreta Concilii prov. Viennensis a. 1858*, tit. IV, cap. X—*Collectio Lacensis*, V, 187; *Decreta Concilii prov. Pragensis a. 1860*, tit. III, cap. XII—*Collectio Lacensis*, V, 484-485; *Decreta Synodi prov. Ultrajectensis, a. 1865*, tit. V, cap. IX—*Collectio Lacensis*, V, 871.

the consent of the ordinary. All authors agree that with regard to the solemn *blessing* of their own churches the authorization of the religious ordinary is required and that in itself it is also sufficient.[51] The authors are equally consonant in declaring that the *consecration* of any church in his diocese, whether it be exempt or not, pertains to the local ordinary.[52] Beste carries this principle to its logical conclusion by stating that, save in the case of a contrary privilege, a religious ordinary who was at the same time a bishop would have to appeal to the local ordinary before he could consecrate even his own proper church.[53] On the other hand, it is wholly conducive to good order that the local ordinary should not consecrate an exempt church without the consent of the exempt superior. Thus canon 1157 protects the rights of the exempt religious superior in his own church and, at the same time, derogates in no way from the authority of the local ordinary as far as the consecration of the church is concerned.[54]

---

[51] Cf. Augustine, *Commentary*, VI, 7; Beste, *Introductio in Codicem*, p. 554; Blat, *De locis et temporibus sacris et de bonis Ecclesiae temporalibus* (2. ed., Romae: Apud Institutum Pontificium Internationale "Angelicum," 1934), pp. 6-7; Claeys Bouuaert-Simenon, *Manuale*, III, 2; Cappello, *Summa Iuris Canonici*, II, 312; Cocchi, *Commentarium*, V, 7; Coronata, *Institutiones*, II, 29, and *idem*, *De Locis et Temporibus Sacris* (Augustae Taurinorum: Marietti, 1922), p. 5; Mayer, *Ordensrecht*, II, 197; Wernz-Vidal, *Ius Canonicum*, IV, pars 1, 441; Woywod, *A Practical Commentary*, II, 2-3; A. Bondini, *De Privilegio Exemptionis* (Romae, 1919), p. 111; J. B. Raus, *Institutiones Canonicae* (2. ed., Paris: Typis Emmanuelis Vittae, 1931), p. 505.

[52] Cf. canon 1155.

[53] *Introductio in Codicem*, p. 553.

[54] Thus Vermeersch-Creusen, *Epitome*, II, 325-326. Ayrinhac (*Administrative Legislation in the New Code of Canon Law* [New York: Longmans, 1930], pp. 3-4), however, holds the opinion that bishops may lawfully consecrate exempt churches even without the consent of the exempt superior: "Some think that a Bishop would need the permission of the superior lawfully to consecrate a church located in his territory but belonging to an exempt order.... This does not, however, seem to be the meaning of this canon." The author does

50. Canon 1164, § 1:

Curent Ordinarii, audito etiam, si opus fuerit, peritorum consilio, ut in ecclesiarum aedificatione vel refectione serventur formae a traditione christiana receptae et artis sacrae leges.

In the erection and restoration of churches, ordinaries should be guided by christian tradition and the rules of sacred art. As is evident, the word *ordinary* here refers to that ecclesiastical superior upon whom the responsibility for the erection and restoration of the church rests. For exempt churches, therefore, it will be the major religious superior.[55]

51. Canon 1165, § 2:

Si prudenter praevideatur ecclesiam conversum iri ad usus profanos, Ordinarius consensum eius aedificationi ne praebeat, aut saltem, si forte aedificata fuerit, eam ne consecret neve benedicat.

If it can be foreseen that the church will be used for profane purposes, the ordinary should not consent to its erection, or at least, if it has already been erected, he should neither consecrate nor bless it. Since the Code says: "saltem, si forte aedificata fuerit, eam . . . neve benedicat", one can imagine a case in which the admonition contained in this canon would be directed to a religious ordinary. As an example showing the reason why the ordinary may be constrained sometimes to refuse to bless or consecrate a church already erected, Coronata[56] gives the following: "Potest periculum profanationis haberi post ecclesiae aedificationem etsi aedificatio legitime facta sit, si eius fundator aut dominus cautiones dare recuset, at casus facilius oc-

---

not offer any specific argument or reason for the opinion which he maintains.

[55] Cf. Blat, *De locis sacris et de bonis Ecclesiae temporalibus*, p. 19; Cocchi, *Commentarium*, V, 24; and Coronata, *Institutiones*, II, 35.

[56] *Institutiones*, II, 38.

curret si aedificatio facta est sine consensu Ordinarii loci." The first of these two cases could obtain with regard to a diocesan church or to one belonging to exempt religious. In the latter event it would be for the religious ordinary neither to invite the local ordinary to consecrate the church nor to bless it himself.

52. **Canon 1169, § 4:**

> **Salvis conditionibus, probante Ordinario, appositis ab illis qui campanam ecclesiae forte dederint, campana benedicta ad usus mere profanos adhiberi nequit, nisi ex causa necessitatis aut ex licentia Ordinarii aut denique ex legitima consuetudine.**

Except in accordance with the stipulations which, with the approval of the ordinary, have been laid down by those who perhaps have presented them to the church, blessed bells must not be rung for any merely profane purpose unless necessity should demand it or unless the ordinary or legitimate custom permit it. When there is question of bells which pertain to a church of exempt clerical religious, the word *ordinary* as here used will refer also to the major superior of that religion. Coronata[57] and Blat[58] expressly hold this opinion. On the other hand, Augustine[59] and Wernz-Vidal[60] restrict the word *ordinary* in this canon to the local ordinary. Wernz-Vidal, as is their custom, appeal to pre-Code legislation in support of their doctrine.

There seems to be little doubt that the local ordinary does have jurisdiction with regard to the ringing of church bells in his diocese, even though they belong to a church of exempt religious. For instance, there is the decree of the

---

[57] *Institutiones*, II, 47, note 8.
[58] *De locis sacris et de bonis Ecclesiae temporalibus*, p. 31 .
[59] *Commentary*, VI, 31-32.
[60] *Ius Canonicum*, IV, pars 1, 530-531.

Sacred Congregation of Rites,[61] which replied in the affirmative to the following question: "An, iubente Ordinario, ut quibusdam Solemnitatibus, vel in alio peculiari casu sonus Aeris Campani omnium Ecclesiarum edatur, praefatae Ecclesiae quantumvis exemptae eius mandato parere teneantur?" The Code itself expresses the same legislation in canon 612. This law, however, by no means excludes all authority of religious ordinaries in this matter. That these latter, together with local ordinaries, should have jurisdiction with regard to the ringing of the bells in their own churches is amply corroborated by Pope Pius V:

> Prohibemus insuper eisdem ordinariis [locorum] ac illis quibuscumque personis, ne impediant ipsos fratres [i.e., religiosos exemptos], quando eis placuerit, tam in diebus dominicis seu festivis aut aliis totius anni temporibus, campanas pulsare . . .[62]

Moreover, if one considers the matter historically, it seems only proper that the ringing of bells in the churches of exempt regulars should be under the jurisdiction of the exempt superior, since it was in the monasteries that bells were first used to call the people to divine service.[63]

53. **Canon 1176:**

> **§ 2. Ecclesiae consecratae valida reconciliatio ad eos spectat de quibus in can. 1156.**
>
> **§ 3. In casu tamen gravis et urgentis necessitatis, si Ordinarius adiri nequeat, rectori ecclesiae consecratae eandem reconciliare fas est, certiore facto postea Ordinario.**

---

[61] Die 3 apr. 1821, ad 3—*Decreta Authentica Congregationis Sacrorum Rituum* (6 vols., Romae, 1898-1927), II, n. 2613; cf. also Wolfgang Mühlbauer, *Decreta Authentica Congregationis Rituum* (4 vols., Monachii, 1865-1867), s. v. "Campanae."

[62] Const. "*Etsi mendicantium*", 16 maii 1567, § 22—*Bullarium Taurinense*, VII, 581.

[63] Cf. E.Vacandard, "Notes sur L'Origine des Cloches,"—*Revue du Clergé Français*, XXIX (1902), 337-355; cf. also Benedict XIV, *Institutiones Ecclesiasticae*, Instit. XX.

The valid reconciliation of a church which has been consecrated pertains either to the local or to the religious ordinary according to the rule prescribed in canon 1156. If, however, a grave and urgent necessity should arise, and the ordinary cannot be consulted, the rector of the church is entitled to perform the rite of reconciliation, but upon using his right he will notify the proper ordinary of the effected reconciliation. All authors who were consulted agree that the ordinary here referred to is, for exempt clerical religious, their own major superior.[64]

54. Canon 1179:

> **Ecclesia iure asyli gaudet ita ut rei, qui ad illam confugerint, inde non sint extrahendi, nisi necessitas urgeat, sine assensu Ordinarii, vel saltem rectoris ecclesiae.**

All churches enjoy the right of asylum so that those who flee to them should not be extradited without necessity unless the ordinary, or at least the rector of the church, shall have given his permission. For the churches of exempt clerical religious, the permission of the major superior should be had, because the canon refers to that ordinary or rector to whose care the church is confided.[65]

---

[64] Cf. Augustine, *Commentary,* VI, 45; Ayrinhac, *Administrative Legislation,* 25; Caesar Badii, *Institutiones Iuris Canonici* (2. ed., Florentiae, 1922), II, 105; Blat, *De locis sacris et de bonis Ecclesiae temporalibus,* p. 41; Claeys Bouuaert-Simenon, *Manuale,* III, 15; Cappello, *Summa Iuris Canonici,* II, 331; Cocchi, *Commentarium,* V, 38; Coronata, *Institutiones,* II, 53; *idem, De Locis Sacris,* 32; Mayer, *Ordensrecht,* II, 196; Pejska, *Ius Canonicum Religiosorum,* p. 255; Schaefer, *De Religiosis,* p. 852; Vermeersch-Creusen, *Epitome,* II, 339; Woywod, *A Practical Commentary,* II, 16; Raus, *Institutiones Canonicae,* p. 510.

[65] Thus Blat, *De Locis sacris et de bonis Ecclesiae temporalibus,* p. 44; Augustine, on the other hand, paraphrases the word *ordinary* here by means of the word *bishop,* thus excluding religious ordinaries; but he gives no special reason for his opinion.

55. Canon 1183:

> **§ 1. Si alii quoque, sive clerici sive laici, in administrationem bonorum alicuius ecclesiae cooptentur, iidem omnes una cum administratore ecclesiastico, de quo in can. 1182, aut eius vicem gerente, eoque praeside, constituant Consilium fabricae ecclesiae.**
>
> **§ 2. Huius Consilii sodales, nisi aliter legitime constitutum fuerit, nominantur ab Ordinario eiusve delegato et ab eodem possunt ob gravem causam removeri.**

If other persons, whether clerics or laymen, are also admitted to participate in the administration of the goods of any church, they shall all form an administrative council of the church together with the ecclesiastical administrator spoken of in Canon 1182 (or his delegate), and under his presidency. Unless other provisions have been legitimately made, the members of this administrative board are to be nominated by the Ordinary or his delegate, and they can be removed by the same person for a grave reason.[66]

If such an administrative board should be chosen for a church belonging to exempt clerical religious, which ordinarily is not done, the right to name and remove the members of this board would pertain to the religious ordinary.[67] However, because of the fact that such a council is not ordinarily formed in the church of a religious organization, this canon is generally considered as referring only to diocesan churches. For this reason also, authors content themselves with the remark that the administration of the goods of an exempt religious church pertains not to the local but to the religious ordinary.[68] Cappello seems to con-

---

[66] Woywod, *A Practical Commentary*, II, 20.

[67] Thus Wernz-Vidal, *Ius Canonicum*, IV, pars 2, 255; also Coronata, *Institutiones*, II, 59.

[68] Cf. Ayrinhac, *Administrative Legislation*, p. 33; Goyeneche, "Consultationes,"—*CpRM*, XII (1931), 367; Schaefer, *De Religiosis* pp. 907-908.

sider that such an administrative board is never erected in a church of exempt religious, for he states that the members of this board must be chosen and removed, unless some particular law provides otherwise, by the local ordinary.[69]

56. Canon 1191, § 2:

> **Quare in oratorio publico, dummodo auctoritate Ordinarii ad publicum Dei cultum perpetuo per benedictionem vel consecrationem, ad normam can. 1155, 1156, dedicatum fuerit, omnes sacrae functiones celebrari possunt, salvo contrario rubricarum praescripto.**

In every public oratory which by the authority of the ordinary has been set aside permanently for the public worship of God by consecration or blessing, all sacred functions permitted by the rubrics can be celebrated. As Augustine[70] rightly remarks: "It may not be amiss to draw attention to the phrase, *auctoritate Ordinarii.* Canons 1155 and 1156 declare that the term *Ordinary* means not only the diocesan bishop, but also the superior of exempt religious. The diocesan bishop has the right to *consecrate* a public oratory, either personally or by a delegate; the superior of exempt religious may *bless* a public oratory in the same way."

57. Canon 1192:

> **§ 1. Oratoria semi-publica erigi nequeunt sine Ordinarii licentia.**
>
> **§ 2. Ordinarius hanc licentiam ne concedat, nisi prius per se vel per alium ecclesiasticum virum oratorium visitaverit et decenter instructum repererit.**

---

[69] *Summa Iuris Canonici,* II, 340.

[70] *Commentary,* VI, 72; and also Cappello, *Summa Iuris Canonici,* II, 350.

§ 3. Data autem licentia, oratorium ad usus profanos converti nequit sine eiusdem Ordinarii auctoritate.

§ 4. In collegiis aut convictibus iuventuti instituendae, in gymnasiis, lyceis, arcibus, praesidiis militum, carceribus, xenodochiis, etc., praeter oratorium principale, alia minora ne erigantur, nisi, Ordinarii iudicio, necessitas aut magna utilitas id exigat.

"Semi-public oratories cannot be erected without the permission of the Ordinary. The Ordinary shall not give this permission before he has inspected, either in person or through another ecclesiastic, the place where the semi-public oratory is to be established, and has convinced himself that the place is decently equipped for the purpose. Once the permission has been granted, the oratory cannot be turned to profane purposes without the authority of the same ordinary. In colleges and other institutions for the education of youths, in high-schools, citadels, barracks of soldiers, prisons, hospices, etc., no other minor oratories should be erected besides the principal one, unless, in the judgment of the ordinary, necessity or great utility makes their erection advisable."[71]

Practically all authors expressly state that the word *ordinary* in this canon does have reference also to religious ordinaries.[72] Several authors propose the question as to

[71] Woywod, *A Practical Commentary,* II, 23.

[72] Cf. A. Arndt, *Die kirchlichen und weltlichen Rechtsbestimmungen für Orden und Kongregationen* (2. ed., Paderborn, 1919), p. 160; Augustine, *Commentary,* VI, 73; Ayrinhac, *Administrative Legislation,* p. 43; Beste, *Introductio in Codicem,* p. 573; Blat, *De locis sacris et de bonis Ecclesiae temporalibus,* p. 62; Claeys Bouuaert-Simenon, *Manuale,* III, 21; Capello, *Summa Iuris Canonici,* II, 351; Cocchi, *Commentarium,* V, 58; Coronata, *Institutiones,* II, 68; *idem, De Locis Sacris,* 78; Goyeneche, "Consultationes,"—*CpRM,* XII (1931), 444-446; Joseph Jansen, *Ordensrecht* (2. ed., Paderborn, 1920), 36; Antonio Jardí, *El Derecho de las Religiosas* (2. ed., Vich, 1927), p. 340;

whether religious ordinaries, in virtue of canon 1192, § 4, can erect semi-public oratories on their farmsteads or at their summer lodges, which in Latin go by the name of *grangiae*. Schaefer holds the opinion that by paragraph four of canon 1192 religious ordinaries are given the power to erect accessory semi-public oratories only in institutes and buildings which are materially, or at least formally, united to the religious house in such a way as to form one whole with it. He concedes, however, that regulars enjoy the privilege granted to the Society of Jesus to erect such chapels in their summer homes and recreational retreats.[73] Augustine[74] takes a more liberal stand and at the same time one which seems to be more in accordance with the Code: "A word may also be said concerning oratories of religious erected on their farms or summer resorts, which in Latin go by the name of *grangiae*, i.e., houses or villas built on the property of religious for sheltering the *oeconomus* or farm boss and his subordinates, hired hands or servants. A laybrother was generally set up as superintendent, and sometimes a priest resided there to say Mass. In modern terms such an oratory would be semi-public, as it serves the convenience of at least a portion of a religious community. Then there are religious institutions which own a college or hospital or university with a chapel insufficient to hold the number of attendants or to permit many priests to say

---

Mayer, *Ordensrecht*, II, 36; Michael Mostaza, "De Potestate Ordinarii Loci in Oratoria Semipublica Religiosorum,"—*Periodica*, XXII (1933), 144-146; Schaefer, *De Religiosis*, pp. 850-851; Vermeersch-Creusen, *Epitome*, II, 350.

[73] Cf. Gregorius XIII, const. "*Decet Romanum*," 3 maii 1575 (as quoted in Ferraris, *Bibliotheca*, s. v. "Oratorium," n. 74): " 'Volumus ut in oratoriis et cappellis quae ipsius Societatis provinciales per se in domibus, collegiis et aliis locis, ubi aliqui Societatis residebunt, approbaverint, et ad divinum dumtaxat cultum deputaverint, missae et alia divina officia, alterius licentia minime requisita, celebrari possint.' "

[74] *Commentary*, VI, 75-76; cf. also Goyeneche, "Consultationes,"—*CpRM*, XII (1931), 444-446; and Wernz-Vidal, *Ius Canonicum*, IV, pars 1, 478.

Mass at a convenient hour. May the superior of these religious grant permission to erect, besides the principal chapel, another accessory one? If the place is owned by the exempt religious their major superior, i.e., the general, provincial, or conventual prior may grant this permission. It is no longer necessary to have recourse to a privilege granted to the Jesuits, or a communication of privileges. Exempt religious superiors are 'Ordinaries' for the purposes of this canon."

A further word should be added concerning paragraph four of this canon. Since this paragraph directly restricts only the number of minor, semi-public oratories that can be erected in schools and other places which are for the benefit primarily of the laity, and since nothing is said of any restriction on the erection of such oratories within a religious house, one may validly presume that the Code wishes to leave the erection of these latter entirely to the discretion of the ordinary and to his prudent judgment as to their necessity or utility.[75]

58. Canon 1193:

> **In oratoriis semi-publicis, legitime erectis, omnia divina officia functionesve ecclesiasticae celebrari possunt, nisi obstent rubricae aut Ordinarius aliqua exceperit.**

In lawfully erected semi-public oratories all sacred and ecclesiastical functions may be celebrated unless the rubrics make some restriction or unless the ordinary prescribe differently.

The word *ordinary* here undoubtedly refers to that ecclesiastical superior who erects the semi-public oratory. Consequently in relation to exempt religious it will be the

---

[75] Cf. Vermeersch-Creusen, *Epitome*, II, 351; Creusen-Garesché-Ellis, *Religious Men and Women in the Code* (3. English ed., Milwaukee: Bruce, 1940), p. 103; Feldhaus, *Oratories* (The Catholic University of America, Canon Law Studies, n. 42, Washington, D. C.: The Catholic University of America, 1927), p. 115.

religious ordinary who may forbid certain sacred functions to be performed in the oratory erected by him.[75*] For this reason one finds it hard to assent to Ayrinhac's translation of this canon: "In legitimately established semi-public chapels all religious functions may be held unless rubrics or special episcopal rulings decide otherwise,"[76] unless the word "episcopal" be interpreted as referring likewise to religious ordinaries.

59. Canon 1195:

§ 1. In oratoriis domesticis ex indulto Apostolicae Sedis, nisi aliud in eodem indulto expresse caveatur, celebrari potest, postquam Ordinarius oratorium visitaverit et probaverit ad normam can. 1192, § 2, unica Missa, eaque lecta, singulis diebus, exceptis festis sollemnioribus; sed aliae functiones ecclesiasticae ibidem ne fiant.

§ 2. Ordinarius vero, dummodo iustae adsint et rationabiles causae, diversae ad eis ob quas indultum concessum fuit, etiam sollemnioribus festis permittere potest per modum actus Missae celebrationem.

In private oratories erected by an Apostolic indult, unless direct provision is made to the contrary, one low Mass may be celebrated on every day except the more solemn feast days, after the ordinary has visited the place and approved it. Augustine[77] and Beste[78] say that such an Apostolic indult is almost invariably addressed to the local ordinary. Consequently Blat[79] says simply that from the context it is

---

[75*] Thus Augustine, *Commentary,* VI, 77; Blat, *De locis sacris et de bonis Ecclesiae temporalibus,* p. 63; Cappello, *Summa Iuris Canonici,* II, 353; Cocchi, *Commentarium,* V, 58; Coronata, *Institutiones,* II, 69; Mayer, *Ordensrecht,* II, 36; Vermeersch-Creusen, *Epitome,* II, 351.

[76] *Administrative Legislation,* p. 44.

[77] *Commentary,* VI, 80.

[78] *Introductio in Codicem,* p. 575.

[79] *De locis sacris et de bonis Ecclesiae temporalibus,* p. 66.

clear that local ordinaries alone are here referred to. If, however, there should occur a case in which such an Apostolic indult was granted to any of those persons who, according to canon 514, are under the jurisdiction of the religious ordinary, this latter and not the local ordinary would be the superior who is properly authorized to visit and approve the place set aside for the oratory.

60. Canon 1200, § 1:

> **Altare immobile amittit consecrationem, si tabula seu mensa a stipite, etiam per temporis momentum, separetur; quo in casu Ordinarius potest permittere ut presbyter altaris consecrationem rursus perficiat ritu formulaque breviore.**

A fixed altar loses its consecration if the table (*tabula seu mensa*) be separated even momentarily from its base. In such a case the ordinary can permit any priest to repeat the rite of consecration by using the shorter form. Vermeersch-Creusen note the fact that this canon brings a new development into Canon Law in that it permits the religious ordinary to provide, either personally or through another priest, for the reconsecration of an altar erected in an exempt church or oratory which has lost its consecration in the above mentioned manner.[80]

61. Canon 1201, § 3:

> **De Ordinarii licentia mutari quidem potest altaris mobilis, non autem altaris immobilis titulus.**

With permission of the ordinary the title of a portable altar, but not the title of a fixed altar, can be changed. There

---

[80] *Epitome*, II, 357; cf. also in the same sense: Beste, *Introductio in Codicem*, p. 579; Blat, *De locis sacris et de bonis Ecclesiae temporalibus*, p. 74; Cappello, *Summa Iuris Canonici*, II, 371; Cocchi, *Commentarium*, V, 72; Coronata, *Institutiones*, II, 82; *idem*, *De Locis Sacris*, p. 114; Mayer, *Ordensrecht*, II, 196; Pejska, *Ius Canonicum Religiosorum*, p. 256.

seems to be no doubt that for altars concerning which he has jurisdiction the religious ordinary can give this permission.[81]

62. Canon 1214:

> **§ 1. Nullum cadaver perpetuae sepulturae ecclesiasticae ubivis traditum exhumare licet, nisi de licentia Ordinarii.**
>
> **§ 2. Ordinarius licentiam nunquam concedat, si cadaver ab aliis corporibus certo discerni nequeat.**

Once a body has been assigned to its final resting place it must not be exhumed without the permission of the ordinary, who must not give such permission unless the body can be distinguished with certainty.

The word *ordinary* refers to that major superior into whose custody the cemetery is confided. To exhume a body, therefore, from the cemeteries of exempt religious the permission of the religious ordinary must be obtained.[82] This is a new development introduced by the Code. Before the appearance of the Code such permission could be given only by the local ordinary. Wernz-Vidal[83] uphold a contrary opinion and say that even now the permission of the local ordinary must be had in all cases. Their chief argument is based on various decrees of the Sacred Congregation of Im-

---

[81] Thus Augustine, *Commentary*, VI, 96, note 46; Blat, *op. cit.*, p. 78: Bliley, *Altars according to the Code of Canon Law* (The Catholic University of America, Canon Law Studies, n. 38, Washington, D. C.: The Catholic University of America, 1927), p. 121; Cappello, *Summa Iuris Canonici*, II, 372; Coronata, *Institutiones*, II, 84; *idem*, *De Locis Sacris*, p. 121.

[82] Thus Ayrinhac, *Administrative Legislation*, p. 67; Blat, *op. cit.*, p. 95; Cappello, *Summa Iuris Canonici*, II, 398; Cocchi, *Commentarium*, V, 101; Coronata, *Institutiones*, II, 95; *idem*, *De Locis Sacris*, p. 153; Raus, *Institutiones Canonicae*, p. 518.

[83] *Ius Canonicum*, IV, pars 1, 681.

munities, especially on those of May 2, 1629, and of August 8, 1645, as quoted in Ferraris.[84]

The law before the Code was very definitely exclusive of religious ordinaries in this matter as is clear from a continuation of the above cited text from Ferraris which reads: "Superioribus vero Regularibus minime licere etiam in Ecclesiis et locis immunibus ipsorum Regularium, sed id ad solos Episcopos spectare;..." i.e., to give permission to exhume a body. However, those who drew up the text of the Code were certainly aware of the then existing legislation on this point and they were also aware of the definite meaning which the word *ordinary* has in the Code. Therefore it appears altogether tenable to assume that they intentionally left out the restrictive word "loci" from this canon in order to include religious ordinaries in so far as their jurisdiction is concerned.

63. Canon 1240:

> **§ 1. Ecclesiastica sepultura privantur, nisi ante mortem aliqua dederint poenitentiae signa:**
>
> **1° Notorii apostatae a christiana fide, aut sectae haereticae vel schismaticae aut sectae massonicae aliisve eiusdem generis societatibus notorie addicti;**
>
> **2° Excommunicati vel interdicti post sententiam condemnatoriam vel declaratoriam;**
>
> **3° Qui se ipsi occiderint deliberato consilio;**
>
> **4° Mortui in duello aut ex vulnere inde relato;**
>
> **5° Qui mandaverint suum corpus cremationi tradi;**

---

[84] *Bibliotheca*, s. v. "Cadaver", nn. 17 and 18: "[Episcopos] non autem posse facultatem concedere eisdem Iudicibus et ministris Laicis in Ecclesiis et aliis locis immunibus ad actum aliquem recognitionis Cadaverum, seu examinis vulneratorum et testium, nisi in casu urgentis necessitatis, et quando Summus Pontifex commode adiri non potest; idque pro eorundem Episcoporum arbitrio recte tamen regulato;..."

6° Alii peccatores publici et manifesti.

§ 2. Occurrente praedictis in casibus aliquo dubio, consulatur, si tempus sinat, Ordinarius; permanente dubio, cadaver sepulturae ecclesiasticae tradatur, ita tamen ut removeatur scandalum.

When there arises a doubt as to whether or not a man must be classed in one of the categories mentioned in paragraph one of this canon and when there is the consequent doubt as to whether he should be granted or refused christian burial, then if time permits the ordinary should be consulted. If time does not permit and the doubt remains, the body should be given christian burial, but care must be taken to obviate all scandal. If the doubt here considered centers about a person subject to a religious ordinary, the religious ordinary will be the one to consult.[85]

64. Canon 1245, § 2:

Ordinarii, ex causa peculiari magni populi concursus aut publicae valetudinis, possunt totam quoque dioecesim seu locum a ieiunio et ab abstinentia vel etiam ab utraque simul lege dispensare.

By reason of a very large concourse of people or for reasons of public health, ordinaries can grant a dispensation from fasting and abstinence to the entire diocese or place. The authors are very equally divided on the question as to whether the word ordinary in this paragraph of canon 1245 may or may not be referred to religious ordinaries. Those who hold the negative opinion base their conclusion chiefly on the context. They argue that although the word *ordinary* is used by itself in this canon, nevertheless from the context it is sufficiently clear that it refers exclusively to local ordinaries.[86] For this opinion militates also the fact

[85] Cf. Coronata, *De Locis Sacris*, p. 268.

[86] Thus Blat, *De locis sacris et de bonis Ecclesiae temporalibus*, pp. 141-142; Claeys Bouuaert-Simenon, *Manuale*, I, 135; Coronata, *Institutiones*, II, 139; Woywod, *A Practical Commentary*, II, 51; *idem*, "Law of the Code on Sacred Seasons,"—*Homiletic and Pastoral Review*, XXVI (1926), 81, 946-954, and 1050.

that the juridical sources for this paragraph as given in the footnote of the Gasparri edition of the Code are all drawn from documents addressed to local ordinaries.[87] Moreover, the canon itself says that the ordinary can grant the dispensation *for the whole diocese or place.* This seems to imply local jurisdiction.

Despite all these reasons, however, the number and authority as well as the arguments of those authors who hold that the word *ordinary* here can be referred also to religious ordinaries are not to be overlooked.[88] The proponents of this opinion argue from the fact that the word *ordinary* is used here without modification despite the fact that in paragraph one there is question of local ordinaries and that in paragraph three religious ordinaries are explicitly included. Therefore, if the legislators had wished to restrict the word, as here used, to local ordinaries, one would have to explain why the definitive word "loci" was omitted. One could argue that the words "diocese" and "place" make unnecessary the use of the word "loci"; but, if one grants that religious ordi-

---

[87] Cf. *Fontes*, nn. 308, 314, 1172, 1176, and 4362.

[88] Cf. Augustine, *Commentary*, VI, 167; Biederlack-Führich, *De Religiosis*, pp. 59-60; Fanfani, *De Iure Religiosorum*, p. 69; and strongest of all Wernz-Vidal, *Ius Canonicum*, III, 111-112: "Principium generale, communiter admissum, erat quod Praelati regulares exempti ea pollebant potestate dispensandi proprios subditos, qua gauderent Episcopi pro suis dioecesanis; atque inferebatur ex Const. S. Pii V "*Romani Pontificis*," 21 Iulii 1571. Codex non retulit eodem modo illud principium, sed distinxit can. 198. inter *Ordinarios loci* et *Ordinarios* et inter hos ultimos accenset omnes Superiores Maiores religionis clericalis exemptae: cum ergo ius tribuit aliquam facultatem Ordinariis, illa pro suis subditis pollent praedicti Superiores maiores, iisdem limitibus circumscripta. Quare v. gr. in vim can. 81 dispensare possunt ex urgente omnino causa ibi descripta; a lege ieiunii et abstinentiae ex causa publicae valetudinis etiam cum integro conventu vel forte integra provincia (in vim can. 1245, § 2). Porro non solum religiosos, inclusis novitiis et postulantibus, sed etiam cum famulis, qui sint commensales et intra domus religiosae septa habitent, cum alumnis seu convictoribus qui a religiosis reguntur, cum hospitibus et infirmis in domo commorantibus. Cit. can. 1245, § 2. et 3. iunct. can. 514, § 1 et 875, § 1."

naries also can be meant here, there is no difficulty in interpreting these two words accordingly, i.e., in the sense that religious ordinaries can exercise this faculty only with regard to those under their jurisdiction.

There is also an argument to be drawn from the constitution "*Romani Pontificis,*"[89] cited by Wernz-Vidal. This Constitution clearly states that religious ordinaries have the same authority over their subjects as local ordinaries have over theirs. Vidal points out that this norm has been given a somewhat new form in canon 198 of the Code. Nevertheless it retains all its vigor for the cases wherein the Code grants to all ordinaries a like power, for example, as happens in canon 1245, § 2, according to the authors above cited. For these reasons also the present writer agrees with this opinion, i.e., religious ordinaries for reasons of public health may dispense an entire province (all those subject to their jurisdiction) from the laws of fast and abstinence by virtue of this canon 1245, § 2.

65. Canon 1279:

> **§ 1. Nemini liceat in ecclesiis, etiam exemptis, aliisve locis sacris ullam insolitam ponere vel ponendam curare imaginem, nisi ab Ordinario loci sit approbata.**
>
> **§ 2. Ordinarius autem sacras imagines publice ad fidelium venerationem exponendas ne approbet, quae cum probato Ecclesiae usu non congruant.**

---

[89] Pius V, 21 Iulii 1571—*Bullarium Taurinense,* VII, 930: "Et insuper, quia sacrum oecumenicum generale Tridentinum concessit episcopis ut absolvere possint in foro animae seu conscientiae ab omnibus peccatis, et dispensare in irregularitatibus, prout sess. XXIV, cap. VI habetur, ne prior conventualis et superiores praelati dicti totius Ordinis, tam in dicta provincia quam extra eam ubilibet, in hac parte deterioris conditionis quam clerici aut saeculares existant, eisdem priori conventuali et superioribus praelatis, ut ipsi per se ipsos idem omnino possint in fratres et moniales dicti Ordinis sibi subiectos, tam quoad absolvendi et dispensandi huiusmodi, quam alias quascumque facultates, eadem auctoritate et tenore, etiam perpetuo concedimus et indulgemus, ac etiam declaramus."

§ 3. Nunquam sinat Ordinarius in ecclesiis aliisve locis sacris exhiberi falsi dogmatis imagines vel quae debitam decentiam et honestatem non praeseferant, aut rudibus periculosi erroris occasionem praebeant.

§ 4. Si imagines, publicae venerationi expositae, sollemniter benedicantur, haec benedictio Ordinario reservatur, qui tamen potest eam cuilibet sacerdoti committere.

Neither in a church, even though it be exempt, nor in any other sacred place, shall any unusual picture be placed unless the local ordinary shall have given his approval. The ordinary shall not thus approve any image unless it conforms to approved ecclesiastical usage. The ordinary must never permit in the churches or other sacred places the exposition of pictures which are inspired by false doctrines, or which are in any way unbecoming, or which may occasion dangerous misconceptions among the people. If sacred images exposed for the veneration of the faithful are to be solemnly blessed, this blessing is reserved to the ordinary, who, however, can delegate it to another priest.

The first three paragraphs of this canon according to their context evidently refer to the local ordinary exclusively.[90] While agreeing to this as far as churches and public oratories are concerned, some authors dissent when there is question of a semi-public oratory which pertains to an exempt clerical religion.[91] They hold that these oratories are subject in this matter to the religious ordinary, in as much as they argue that the phrase "etiam exemptis" of paragraph one, since it comes after the word "ecclesiis" and

---

[90] Cf. Raus, *Institutiones Canonicae*, p. 533, note 1; Schaefer, *De Religiosis*, p. 888; Vermeersch-Creusen, *Epitome*, II, 425; and also Ferraris, *Bibliotheca*, s. v. "Imagines," n. 10.

[91] Cf. Blat, *De locis sacris et de bonis Ecclesiae temporalibus*, p. 207; Coronata, *Institutiones*, II, 183; Pejska, *Ius Canonicum Religiosorum*, p. 321.

before the phrase "aliisve locis sacris," has reference only to churches and public oratories. Such an opinion, however, can hardly stand upon a comparison of this canon with the source from which it was taken, i.e., with the ruling of the Council of Trent, which extended the bishop's power to include also the above mentioned semi-public oratories.[92]

With regard to the solemn blessing of images which is mentioned in canon 1279, § 4, religious ordinaries, according to the norm given in canon 1156, have the same authority as local ordinaries, provided there is question of an image exposed in a church or oratory under their jurisdiction.[93]

66. Canon 1280:

> **Imagines pretiosae, idest vetustate, arte, aut cultu praestantes, in ecclesiis vel oratoriis publicis fidelium venerationi expositae, si quando reparatione indigeant, nunquam restaurentur sine dato scriptis consensu ab Ordinario; qui, antequam licentiam concedat, prudentes ac peritos viros consulat.**

"Precious images—that is to say, those that are conspicuous for their antiquity, art, or veneration—exposed for the public veneration of the faithful in churches and public oratories must, when in need of repairs, be restored only after the obtaining of the written consent of the ordinary,

---

[92] Sess. XXV, "De Invocatione, veneratione, et Reliquiis Sanctorum, et sacris imaginibus," ad finem: "Haec ut fidelibus observentur, statuit sancta Synodus, nemini licere ullo in loco, vel Ecclesia, etiam quomodolibet exempta, ullam insolitam ponere vel ponendam curare imaginem, nisi ab Episcopo approbata fuerit; nulla etiam admittenda esse nova miracula, nec novas Reliquias recipiendas, nisi eodem recognoscente et approbante Episcopo, qui simul atque de iis aliquod compertum habuerit, adhibitis in consilium Theologis, et aliis piis viris, ea faciat, quae veritati et pietati consentanea judicaverit."

[93] Cf. Beste, *Introductio in Codicem*, p. 632; Blat, *op. cit.*, p. 208; Bondini, *De Privilegio Exemptionis*, p. 120; Bonzelet, *The Pastoral Companion* (8. ed., Chicago: Franciscan Herald Press, 1939), p. 208; Cocchi, *Commentarium,* V, 211; Coronata, *Institutiones,* II, 183; Mayer, *Ordensrecht,* II, 196; Schaefer, *De Religiosis*, p. 888; Raus, *Institutiones Canonicae,* p. 533, note 1.

who before giving the permission shall seek prudent and expert advice in the matter."[94]

All authors agree that with relation to precious images which are exposed in churches or oratories of exempt clerical religions, the competent superior is the religious ordinary.[95]

67. Canon 1303, § 2:

> **Si qua ecclesia paupertate laboret, potest Ordinarius permittere ut a sacerdotibus qui in proprium commodum inibi celebrant, propter utensilia ceteraque ad Missae sacrificium necessaria, moderata stipes exigatur.**

If a church is impoverished the ordinary may permit, but only in order to care for the incurred expenses, that a moderate tax or fee be exacted from priests who for their own personal convenience celebrate the Holy Sacrifice therein.

Although some authors leave out all mention of religious ordinaries by putting "ordinarius loci" or "episcopus" for the canon's "ordinarius",[96] nevertheless it seems more in accordance with the Code to hold that, unless the bishop or a legitimate custom has already established the amount of such a tax, it would be permitted for the religious ordinary to do so in connection with the churches which are under his jurisdiction.[97] In favor of this opinion stands the fact

[94] Woywod, *A Practical Commentary,* II, 72-73.

[95] Cf. Beste, *Introductio in Codicem,* p. 632; Blat, *op. cit.,* p. 209; Cocchi, *Commentarium,* V, 211; Coronata, *Institutiones,* II, 184; Larraona, "Commentarium Codicis,"—*CpRM,* XIII (1932), 354, note 654; Pejska, *Ius Canonicum Religiosorum,* p. 322; Raus, *Institutiones Canonicae,* p. 533; Schaefer, *De Religiosis,* p. 888; Vermeersch-Creusen, *Epitome,* II, 425.

[96] Cf. Cappello, *Summa Iuris Canonici,* II, 378-379; *idem, De Sacramentis,* I, 750; Wernz-Vidal, *Ius Canonicum,* IV, pars 1, 515.

[97] Thus Beste, *Introductio in Codicem,* p. 640; Cocchi, *Commentarium,* V, 241-242; Stadtmüller, *Das neue Ordensrecht,* 140, note 9; Vermeersch-Creusen, *Epitome,* II, 438.

that the Code here employs the word *ordinary* without modification. Moreover, before the appearance of the Code not only religious ordinaries but all ecclesiastical administrators of churches or shrines had this power.[98]

68. Canon 1341, § 1:

> **Sacerdotes extradioecesani sive saeculares sive religiosi ad concionandum ne invitentur, nisi prius licentia ab Ordinario loci in quo concio habenda sit, obtenta fuerit; hic autem, nisi eorum idoneitatem aliunde compertam habeat, licentiam ne concedat, nisi prius bonum testimonium super concionatoris doctrina, pietate, moribus a proprio eiusdem Ordinario habuerit; qui, graviter onerata conscientia, secundum veritatem respondere tenetur.**

Extra-diocesan priests, be they secular or religious, must not be invited to preach without the previous permission of the ordinary of the place wherein the sermon is preached. For his part the local ordinary is cautioned not to grant this permission before he has received from the proper ordinary of the prospective preacher a favorable testimonial letter concerning his doctrinal knowledge, his piety, and his character. When there is question of giving this testimonial to a member of an exempt clerical religion, the major superior is the competent ordinary. This is clear from the instruction of the Sacred Congregation of the Consistory of June 28, 1917.[99] Augustine,[100] according to the example that he proposes, demands that a member of a clerical exempt re-

---

[98] Cf. Augustinus Lehmkuhl, *Theologia Moralis* (12. ed., 2 vols., Friburgi Brisgoviae, 1914), II, 160 and 164.

[99] "Norma pro Sacra Praedicatione," cap. I, n. 11—*AAS*, IX (1917), 328; cf. also *Periodica*, IX (1921), 31-43; the following authors hold the same opinion: Ayrinhac, *Administrative Legislation*, p. 217; Blat, *op. cit.*, p. 302; Pejska, *Ius Canonicum Religiosorum*, p. 279; Vermeersch-Creusen, *Epitome*, II, 468.

[100] *Commentary*, VI, 360.

ligion must get his testimonial letter from the local ordinary of the diocese within which is situated the house with which the religious is affiliated. This cannot, however, be agreed to in view of the above mentioned instruction of the Sacred Consistorial Congregation. The reason is that, for clerics of exempt clerical religions, the *proper* ordinary is their major superior and not the local ordinary, except in the cases expressly mentioned in the Code.

69. Canon 1342, § 1:

> **Concionandi facultas solis sacerdotibus vel diaconis fiat, non vero ceteris clericis, nisi rationabili de causa, iudicio Ordinarii et in casibus singularibus.**

Faculties for preaching may be granted only to priests or deacons, not to other clerics, unless a reasonable cause in the judgment of the ordinary should persuade a departure from this rule in some particular case. Wernz-Vidal,[101] in commenting on this canon, replace the phrase "iudicio Ordinarii" of the text with the phrase "ex licentia Episcopi," thus excluding religious ordinaries from any competence in this matter. Ordinarily, it is true, it will be the local ordinary who must be consulted; but, if the sermon is to be given only to exempt religious, the major superior, on the strength of canon 1338, § 1, will be the proper ordinary to give the necessary permission.

70. Canon 1344:

> **§ 2. Parochus huic obligationi (praedicandi diebus dominicis) nequit per alium habitualiter satisfacere, nisi ob iustam causam ab Ordinario probatam.**
>
> **§ 3. Potest Ordinarius permittere ut sollemnioribus quibusdam festis aut etiam, ex iusta causa, aliquibus diebus dominicis concio omittatur.**

---

[101] *Ius Canonicum,* IV, pars 2, 32-33.

The obligation which the parish priest has of announcing the word of God to his flock on Sundays and Holy Days cannot be satisfied habitually through another priest except by reason of a just cause approved by the ordinary. The ordinary can permit that the sermon be omitted on the more solemn feast days and even on some Sundays if there is a just cause for it. From the context it is evident that the word *ordinary* in this canon refers only to local ordinaries[102] since they alone can give the permission which is required before one may preach to the people of the diocese.

71. **Canon 1349, § 1:**

Ordinarii advigilent ut, saltem decimo quoque anno, sacram, quam vocant, missionem, ad gregem sibi commissum habendam parochi curent.

Ordinaries should take care that the pastors provide missions for their parishioners at least once every ten years. Since this is a matter which has for its end the spiritual welfare of the parishioners, the obligation of seeing that such missions are given belongs exclusively to the local ordinary. Even in the case of a pastor who is an exempt religious, if the religious ordinary should insist that these missions be held, he will not be acting on the strength of this present canon, but rather as a religious superior who has dominative power over his subjects. For this reason the writer cannot agree with the opinion proposed by Blat,[103] which regards the authority of the religious ordinary to be of the same nature as that which the local ordinary has, as far as exempt religious pastors are concerned. As Bondini

---

[102] Cf. Blat. *op. cit.*, p. 307; and Pejska, *Ius Canonicum Religiosorum*, p. 281.

[103] *Op. cit.*, p. 314; "Novum est in iure communi praescriptum can. 1349, § 1. *Ordinarii* locorum ex contextu atque simul Superior maior, quando parochus fuerit religiosus exemptus, *advigilent*, qua pastorale officium, *ut, saltem decimo quoque anno, . . . sacram, quam vocant, missionem . . . . ad gregem sibi . . . . commissum habendam . . . parochi curent.*"

says, this is a matter in which all religious are absolutely dependent on the local ordinary.[104]

72. Canon 1363, § 1:

> **In Seminarium ab Ordinario ne admittantur, nisi filii legitimi quorum indoles et voluntas spem afferant eos cum fructu ecclesiasticis ministeriis perpetuo inserviturcs.**

The ordinary should see to it that none will be admitted into the seminary except such as have been born of lawful wedlock and whose endowments, character, and intentions provide the hope that they will consecrate themselves permanently and with fruitful service to the sacred ministry. Undoubtedly in the majority of cases it will be the local ordinary who must watch over the type of candidates admitted into the major or minor seminary. However, in a seminary which pertains to an exempt religion, this office will rest on the shoulders of the religious ordinary also. For students who are admitted into the seminary with the express intention of embracing the religious life subsequently in that community, the obligation here considered will rest with the religious ordinary.[105]

A number of authors,[106] when commenting on this canon, do not take into consideration the possibility of its application to religious ordinaries. Consequently they transcribe the word "Ordinarius" of the Code by the word "Episcopus" or "Ordinarius loci" and thus exclude religious ordinaries. As long, however, as these authors give no special reason for such exclusion the contrary opinion expressed by Gerster a Zeil remains the more probable.

---

[104] *De Privilegio Exemptionis*, p. 131: "In hac igitur materia Regulares, si habeant ecclesias paroeciales, ab Ordinario loci totaliter pendent."

[105] Cf. Gerster a Zeil, *Ius Religiosorum*, p. 201.

[106] Cf. Blat, *op. cit.*, p. 338; Cocchi, *Commentarium*, VI, 97-98; and Coronata, *Institutiones*, II, 290.

73. Canon 1397, § 5:

Libros qui subtilius examen exigant vel de quibus ad salutarem effectum consequendum supremae auctoritatis sententia requiri videatur, ad Apostolicae Sedis iudicium Ordinarii deferant.

Books which require a profoundly scrutinizing examination or which need condemnation by the supreme authority in order to beget the desired salutary effect should be sent by the ordinary for judgment to the Holy See. The scrutiny of the books spoken of here clearly falls within the jurisdiction of the local ordinary according to the ruling expressed in the previous paragraph of canon 1397. Therefore local ordinaries certainly have the obligation of sending a copy of such books to the Holy See as soon as they appear.[107]

However, since 1.) this sending of the book to the Holy See is not an act of jurisdiction, and since 2.) the word here used is *ordinary* and not *local ordinary,* and since 3.) the chief purpose of this law is that a copy of such books *should be sent* to the Holy See, it seems not at all contrary either to the wording or to the spirit of the Code to hold that religious ordinaries also should keep their eyes open on this point and, if they encounter a book falling into the above category, send it for judgment to Rome,[108] or refer it to the local ordinary so that he may forward it to Rome. Nevertheless the obligation which is incumbent on a religious ordinary in this matter does not derive from canon 1397, § 5, but rather from the position of responsibility in which he is constituted as a major superior of an exempt clerical religion.

---

[107] Cf. Blat, *op. cit.,* p. 404; Wernz-Vidal, *Ius Canonicum,* IV, pars 2, 159.

[108] Thus Augustine, *Commentary,* VI, 463; and Pernicone, *The Ecclesiastical Prohibition of Books* (The Catholic University of America, Canon Law Studies, n. 72, Washington, D. C.: The Catholic University of America, 1932), p. 101, note 29.

74. Canon 1401:

S. R. E. Cardinales, Episcopi, etiam titulares, aliique Ordinarii, necessariis adhibitis cautelis, ecclesiastica librorum prohibitione non adstringuntur.

Cardinals, all bishops, and other ordinaries, provided they employ the necessary safeguards, are not bound by the law regarding the ecclesiastical prohibition of books. All authors agree that among the *other ordinaries* of the canon are included major superiors of exempt clerical religions.[109]

75. Canon 1402, § 1:

Ordinarii licentiam, ad libros quod attinet ipso iure vel decreto Sedis Apostolicae prohibitos, concedere suis subditis valent pro singulis tantum libris atque in casibus dumtaxat urgentibus.

"In the case of books forbidden by the general law of the Church or by Decree of the Holy See, Ordinaries can give their subjects permission to read only individual books and in urgent cases only."[110]

As with the foregoing canon, authors are unanimous in applying this canon also to religious ordinaries in so far as their jurisdiction extends.[111]

---

[109] Cf. Augustine, *Commentary*, VI, 478; Blat, *op. cit.*, p. 416; Cappello, *Summa Iuris Canonici*, II, 469; Cocchi, *Commentarium*, VI, 170; Coronata, *Institutiones*, II, 345; Melo, *De Exemptione Regularium*, p. 70; Pejska, *Ius Canonicum Religiosorum*, p. 175; Pernicone, *The Ecclesiastical Prohibition of Books*, p. 197; Schaefer, *De Religiosis*, p. 884; Raus, *Institutiones Canonicae*, p. 561; and Woywod, *A Practical Commentary*, II, 132.

[110] Woywod, *A Practical Commentary*, II, 132.

[111] Cf. Augustine, *Commentary*, VI, 479; *idem*, *Rights and Duties of Ordinaries*, 353; Blat, *op. cit.*, p. 417; Cappello, *Summa Iuris Canonici*, II, 469; Cocchi, *Commentarium*, VI, 171; Coronata, *Institutiones*, II, 346; Creusen-Garesche-Ellis, *Religious Men and Women in the Code*, p. 45; D'Angelo, *La Esenzione dei Religiosi nella vigente disciplina ecclesiastica* (Torino, 1922), p. 54; Mayer, *Ordensrecht*, II, 180; Melo, *De Exemptione Regularium*, p. 70; Pejska,

76. **Canon 1403, § 1:**

Qui facultatem apostolicam consecuti sunt legendi et retinendi libros prohibitos, nequeunt ideo et legere et retinere libros quoslibet a suis Ordinariis proscriptos, nisi in apostolico indulto expressa iisdem facta fuerit potestas legendi et retinendi libros a quibuslibet damnatos.

"Persons who have obtained from the Holy See the permission to read and keep forbidden books cannot for that reason read and keep books forbidden by their own Ordinaries, unless the Apostolic indult explicitly grants them the faculty to read and keep books forbidden by *any* authority."[112] Pernicone rightly applies this canon to religious by stating that an exempt regular who has Apostolic permission may read works condemned by the local ordinary, but not those condemned by his own ordinary, unless the opposite is expressly stated in the indult.[113]

77. **Canon 1406, § 1:**

Obligatione emittendi professionem fidei, secundum formulam a Sede Apostolica probatam, tenentur:

8° Coram Ordinario eiusve delegato Rector Universitatis vel Facultatis; coram Rectore vero Universitatis vel Facultatis eiusve delegato, professores omnes in Universitate seu Facultate canonice erecta, initio cuiusque anni scholastici vel saltem initio suscepti muneris; itemque qui, periculo facto, academicis gradibus donantur.

Ius Canoicum Religiosorum, p. 175; Pernicone, *The Ecclesiastical Prohibition of Books,* p. 200; Schaefer, *De Religiosis,* p. 884; Vermeersch-Creusen, *Epitome,* II, 517; Wernz-Vidal, *Ius Canonicum,* IV, pars 2, 174; Woywod, "Prohibition of Books,"—*Homiletic and Pastoral Review,* XXVIII (1928), 1086-1095.

[112] Woywod, *A Practical Commentary,* II, 132.

[113] *The Ecclesiastical Prohibition of Books,* p. 206; cf. also Augustine, *Commentary,* VI, 481; and Schaefer, *Re Religiosis,* pp. 884-885.

The rector of a Catholic University or Faculty is bound to make the profession of faith before the ordinary or his delegate according to the form approved by the Holy See. Augustine,[114] Cocchi[115] and Woywod[116] change the import of the canon by stating that the rector must make the profession of faith before the *local* ordinary. They do so despite the fact that the word "loci" is absent from this number in the text of the Code. In the three preceding numbers, 5, 6, and 7, it is expressly mentioned. Therefore, it seems logical to assume that the legislator omitted the word "loci" here for a special purpose. That purpose is easily understood if one adverts to the fact that many Universities and Faculties have been given in charge to one or the other religious community. If it be a clerical exempt community the rector will make his profession of faith before the religious ordinary of that religion.[117]

78. Canons 1409-1447 and 1472-1488:

CONCERNING ECCLESIASTICAL BENEFICES:

Canon 1414:

§ 1. Beneficia consistorialia una Sedes Apostolica erigit.

§ 2. Praeter Romanum Pontificem, Ordinarii in suo quisque territorio beneficia non consistorialia erigere possunt, salvo praescripto can. 394, § 2.

§ 3. Attamen Vicarii Generales nequeunt beneficia erigere nisi ex peculiari mandato.

§ 4. Etiam Cardinalis in proprio titulo vel diaconia potest beneficia non curata erigere, nisi ecclesia sit religionis clericalis exemptae.

---

[114] *Commentary,* VI, 489.

[115] *Commentarium,* VI, 181-182.

[116] *A Practical Commentary,* II, 134.

[117] Thus Blat, *op. cit.,* p. 426.

Canon 1432:

§ 1. Ad collationem beneficiorum vacantium, Cardinalis in proprio titulo vel diaconia et Ordinarius loci in proprio territorio habent intentionem in iure fundatam.

§ 2. Conferre autem beneficia nequit Vicarius Generalis sine speciali mandato; Vicarius autem Capitularis nec paroecias vacantes, nisi ad normam can. 455, § 2, n. 3, neque alia beneficia perpetua liberae collationis.

§ 3. Si Ordinarius intra semestre ab habita certa vacationis notitia beneficium non contulerit, huius collatio devolvitur ad Sedem Apostolicam, salvo praescripto can. 458.

These two canons which treat of the erecting and the conferring of benefices furnish the fundamental legislation with regard to their administration. As is clear, if one acknowledges the right of the religious ordinary to erect or to confer certain benefices, to him likewise will pertain the consequent rights and duties enumerated in the various canons.[118]

First of all the principle is established and acknowledged in all the Code's legislation that religious ordinaries have no authority of themselves to erect benefices which are concerned with the care of souls. With regard to the conferring of these benefices, even though the religious ordinary may have the right of presentation or nomination, nevertheless the "institutio auctorizabilis," i.e., the actual giving of jurisdiction for the care of souls, pertains always and exclusively to the local ordinary.[119] As a general principle,

---

[118] Cf. especially canons 1415, § 1; 1417, § 1; 1426; 1432, § 3; and 1444, § 1.

[119] Cf. for pre-Code legislation on this point, the Council of Trent, sess. XXI, *de ref.*, c. 4; sess. XXIV, *de ref.*, c. 18; cf. also Ferraris, *Bibliotheca*, s. v. "Beneficium," art. I, nn. 8-9; art. II, nn. 1, 5, 8; art. III, n. 98; s. v. "Vicarius Parochialis," n. 46; and Anacletus

therefore, it is evident that with regard to *beneficia curata* religious ordinaries according to the general law of the Code have no jurisdiction.

In the following discussion the question will deal with *beneficia non curata* exclusively. Has the religious ordinary jurisdiction with regard to these? Can he of his own authority canonically erect such a benefice? If it be erected as a religious benefice, has he then the right of conferring it?[120]

There are 54 canons under the title "De Beneficiis Ecclesiasticis" in the Code: 1409-1447 and 1472-1488. In these canons there are only 14 instances of the use of the word *ordinary* standing by itself. If one were to take into consideration the law simply as stated in the Code, one would be forced to conclude that the word *ordinary* in all of these 14 cases refers exclusively to local ordinaries. One would likewise come to the same conclusion by simply reading the authors who comment on these canons.[121]

Even when commenting on canon 1411, n. 2, which speaks of secular and *religious* benefices, and on canon 1442, which states that secular benefices are to be conferred on seculars

---

Reiffenstuel, *Ius Canonicum Universum* (Iuxta Novissimam Romanam editionem ... cui ... accedunt ... adnotationes ... digestae studio et opera R. D. Pelletier, 5 vols. in 7, Parisiis, 1864-1882), lib. III, tit. V, n. 102. For post-Code authors cf. Coronata, *Institutiones*, II, 388; and Wernz-Vidal, *Ius Canonicum*, II, 176.

[120] Cf. what has already been written on religious offices, n. 20 *supra* pp. 37-40.

[121] More than 20 authors were consulted. Among all of these, however, only one instance was found in which an author said expressly that religious ordinaries could be understood as being included under the term *ordinary* in any one of the canons studied: Augustine, *Commentary*, VI, 499: "Can. 1417 permits the founder to lay down *certain conditions* in the charter with the *consent of the ordinary*, i.e., the diocesan bishop or the superior of exempt clerical religious if the benefice is to be a religious one." All the other authors, and even Augustine with regard to all the rest of the canons, write their commentaries for local ordinaries, leaving out all references to religious, as they also leave out, though to a lesser degree, all mention of *non curata* benefices.

and religious benefices on religious, the authors never mention a word about the ecclesiastical authority who erects religious benefices nor on whom devolves the right to confer them.[122] Consequently, one would be led to conclude that the erection of all benefices in an exempt clerical religion, even of those which have not the care of souls, pertains to the local ordinary, unless, of course, the religious ordinary can claim this right by virtue of a legitimate custom, privilege, or special Apostolic indult. What is said here concerning the erection of religious benefices will obtain likewise in the conferring of these same benefices.[123]

Despite this, however, there does arise a serious doubt as to whether this almost common opinion reflects the correct doctrine. The following reasons would rather incline one to the opinion that, with regard to the *beneficia non curata* which are erected within an exempt clerical community, the religious ordinary is the competent authority.

1.) The first argument is taken from canon 1414, § 4, which says that Cardinals in their own titular churches can erect benefices to which no care of souls is attached *provided that the church does not pertain to an exempt clerical*

---

[122] It is to be recalled that the question here concerns only the *beneficia non curata.* Both the Code and the authors give ample treatment to the question of the *beneficia curata.*

[123] Ferraris, *Bibliotheca,* s. v. "Beneficium," nn. 1 and 5: "Beneficia ecclesiastica debent erigi cum auctoritate expressa episcopi.... Neque ad canonicam erectionem beneficii ecclesiastici sufficit auctoritas praelati inferioris, qui iura episcopi non habet, quamvis sit exemptus et nullius." Cf. also *Dictionnaire de Droit Canonique,* s. v. "Bénéfices: Droit Commun D'Après Le Code", II, 686: "Le Canon [1432] parle de *l'Ordinarius loci,* par quoi on doit entendre, non seulement les évêques mais encore les abbés et prélats *nullius,* les administrateurs apostoliques, les vicaires et préfets apostoliques (can. 198, § 1), a l'exclusion des supérieurs religieux." Cf. also Wernz-Vidal, *Ius Canonicum,* II, 176: "Episcopus sive Ordinarius loci, excluso Vicario Generali speciali mandato non munito, ad erigenda omnia alia beneficia vel officia ecclesiastica inferiora seu non consistorialia, quae secundum disciplinam Ecclesiae nunc vigentem institui solent, solus competens est, non alii inferiores Praelati etiam exempti absque suffragio Episcopi dioecesani aut sine speciali privilegio Sedis Apostolicae."

religion. Why should this restriction be placed on the power of Cardinals except to show that the erection of such benefices in these churches belongs to the exempt ordinary of that religion? Pistocchi says: "Quoad alia beneficia, ideo non erigit Cardinalis, si ecclesia sit religionis clericalis exemptae, quia in hac hypothesi beneficia erecta, sunt ordinarie religiosa, et non secularia."[124] Therefore, unless it be supposed that the Holy See reserves to itself the erecting and conferring of all *non curata* benefices in clerical exempt communities, which seems improbable, one is forced to conclude that such benefices are subject exclusively to the religious ordinary.

2.) A second argument may be taken from the fact that before the Code the conferring at least of *non curata* benefices pertained by custom to the religious ordinary.[125] There is question here of a "ius quaesitum" which is not revoked expressly by the Code; hence, according to canon 4, it is still in effect.

3.) Augustine and Blat seem to hold this opinion. Augustine, as above stated, says that when the benefice is to be a religious one, the right to assent to the conditions proposed in the foundation belongs according to canon 1417 to the religious ordinary. Blat describes an exempt benefice as one the conferring of which does not pertain to the local

---

[124] *De Re Beneficiali Iuxta Canones* (Taurini, 1928), p. 47; cf. also *Dictionnaire de Droit Canonique,* s. v. "Bénéfices: Droit Commun D'Après Le Code," II, 678: "De plus les cardinaux ne peuvent pas ériger de bénéfice dans une église de religion cléricale exempte (can. 1414), parce que dans ce cas le bénéfice est ordinairement religieux et que le régle est: *religiosa religiosis.*" In other words the erection of a benefice in the church of an exempt religious community pertains to the religious, i.e., to the competent religious superior.

[125] Cf. *Dictionnaire de Droit Canonique,* s. v. "Bénéfice Ecclésiastiques en Occident: 1. Le Régime de Droit Commun, des Origines au Concordat de Vienne (1448)," II, 416: "La Collation des bénéfices réguliers (offices claustraux, prieurés non conventuels, celles, etc.) et des séculiers dépendant de communautés religieuses appartenait soit à l'abbé seul, soit conjointement à ses moines, soit exclusivement à ses derniers."

ordinary: "*Beneficia exempta* proinde non conferenda per loci Ordinarium. . ."[126]

These three arguments linked with the principle of canons 615 and 618 relative to the power of local ordinaries in religious communities form the basis of a solidly probable opinion which acknowledges the authority of religious ordinaries both to erect and to confer *non curata* religious benefices.

The following four conclusions sum up what has here been said concerning benefices:

1.) All *curata* benefices, whether secular or religious, are altogether under the jurisdiction of the local ordinary with regard both to their erection and also to their conferring, although the right of presentation may belong to a religious ordinary.

2.) *Non curata* religious benefices erected in a church or house of an exempt clerical religion are altogether under the jurisdiction of the religious ordinary both as to their erection and also as to their conferring, and this by virtue of immemorable custom which has established this right for them.

3.) Nowadays, however, *non curata* benefices are rarely erected. Therefore, in this country especially, the question will have no practical importance. Whenever an occasion for founding a *non curatum* benefice presents itself, the religious ordinary, if he does not wish to erect a benefice, may establish a pious foundation according to canons 1544-1551. This will be the ordinary procedure because of the fact that the practice of founding *non curata* benefices has practically fallen into desuetude in modern times.

4.) Since the erection of *non curata* benefices is a comparatively rare thing in present day Church discipline and since religious ordinaries of themselves have no authority either to erect or confer *curata* benefices, all the canons of this section which without modification employ the word

[126] *De locis sacris et de bonis Ecclesiae temporalibus* (1923), p. 401.

ordinary will be placed in that group of canons in which the religious ordinary can have no authority according to the general law of the Code.

79. Canons 1448-1471:

THE RIGHT OF PATRONAGE

Much that has been said in the foregoing number 78 will find application also with regard to these canons. Undoubtedly the Code looks upon the right of patronage as being under the special vigilance of the local ordinary to the exclusion of the religious ordinary. If, however, the right of patronage still exists with regard to any religious benefice which by custom or Apostolic indult is subject entirely to the religious ordinary, the competent ecclesiastical authority to moderate this right of patronge will be this same religious ordinary. Practically, however, such cases do not occur, or at least they occur only rarely; therefore, the eight canons in this section which use the word *ordinary* without any modification are all considered as referring simply to the local ordinary.

80. Canon 1503:

> **Salvis praescriptis can. 621-624, vetantur privati tam clerici quam laici sine Sedis Apostolicae aut proprii Ordinarii et Ordinarii loci licentia, in scriptis data, stipem cogere pro quolibet pio aut ecclesiastico instituto vel fine.**

Save for the prescriptions laid down in canons 621-624, all private persons, whether clerical or lay, are forbidden to collect money for any pious or ecclesiastical institute or purpose unless they have permission from the Holy See or from their own proper ordinary and the ordinary of the place where they make the collection. The law is, therefore, that in order to collect money in a diocese for any religious purpose at all, one must have the permission of the Holy See or of his own proper ordinary and of the ordinary of the place where the money is collected. For their own subjects the religious ordinary is the proper ordinary referred to in the canon.[127] Religious who belong to mendicant orders do not need the permission of the local ordinary of the diocese in which their house is situated, as is clear from canon 621.[128]

81. Canon 1506:

Aliud tributum in bonum dioecesis vel pro patrono imponere ecclesiis, beneficiis aliisque institutis ecclesiasticis, quanquam sibi subiectis, Ordinarius potest tantummodo in actu fundationis vel consecrationis; sed nullum imponi tributum potest super eleemosynis Missarum sive manualium sive fundatarum.

Besides the taxes mentioned in canon 1505, the ordinary can exact no other tax either for the good of the diocese or in favor of a patron from any church or benefice except at the time of the drawing up of the decree of foundation or at the time of the consecration of the church; no taxes, however, can ever be placed on Mass stipends, whether they be manual or founded.

This canon refers only to local ordinaries as is indicated from the two preceding canons and the one following, although in the Decretals of Gregory IX this prohibition embraced religious ordinaries also.[129]

By analogy this canon could be made to apply also to religious ordinaries, but as it stands and in consideration of

---

[127] Cf. Ayrinhac, *Administrative Legislation,* p. 394.

[128] Cf. Maroto, "Annotationes,"—*CpRM,* I (1920), 169-171; and Schaefer, *De Religiosis,* p. 804.

[129] Cf. c. 7, X, *de censibus, exactionibus et procurationibus,* III, 39: "Prohibemus insuper, ne ab abbatibus, episcopis, vel aliis praelatis, novi census imponantur ecclesiis, nec veteres augeantur, nec partem redditum suis usibus appropriare praesumant; sed libertatem quam sibi maiores conservare desiderant, minoribus suis, bona voluntate conservent." Cf. also c. un., *de excessibus praelatorum,* V, 6, in Clem.

the entire context it can hardly be held that this canon refers to any but local ordinaries.

82. Canon 1515:

> **§ 1. Ordinarii omnium piarum voluntatum tam mortis causa quam inter vivos exsecutores sunt.**
>
> **§ 2. Hoc ex iure Ordinarii vigilare possunt, ac debent, etiam per visitationem, ut piae voluntates impleantur, et alii exsecutores delegati debent, perfuncti munere, illis reddere rationem.**
>
> **§ 3. Clausulae huic Ordinariorum iuri contrariae, ultimis voluntatibus adiectae, tanquam non appositae habeantur.**

Ordinaries are the canonically appointed executors of all pious donations and bequests. Therefore the ordinaries can and must watch over the fulfillment of these donations even by means of canonical visitation; all other delegated executors must, when they have fulfilled their duty, give an account of what they have done to the ordinary. All clauses in last wills contrary to this right of ordinaries must be ignored. Although Blat[130] is of the opinion that the ordinary here referred to will always be the local ordinary, since those who make such donations are always subject to a bishop, nevertheless the Code simply says *ordinaries*. Moreover, the two following canons which treat of the same matter most certainly refer also to religious ordinaries, i.e., when the object of the donation or bequest pertains to his jurisdiction.[131]

---

[130] *De locis sacris et de bonis Ecclesiae temporalibus*, p. 580.

[131] Cf. Augustine, *Commentary*, VI, 573; Ayrinhac, *Administrative Legislation*, p. 417; Beste, *Introductio in Codicem*, p. 735; Cappello, *Summa Iuris Canonici*, III, 31; Cocchi, *Commentarium*, VI, 379; Coronata, *Institutiones*, II, 466; Gerster a Zeil, *Ius Religiosorum*, p. 51; Jerome Hannan, *The Canon Law of Wills* (The Catholic University of America, Canon Law Studies, n. 86, Washington, D. C.: The Catholic University of America, 1934), p. 451; Nebreda, "Quaestiones Selectae de Iure Administrativo Ecclesiastico,"—*CpRM*, VII (1926), 327; Schaefer, *De Religiosis*, p. 1044; Vermeersch-Creusen,

83. Canon 1516:

§ 1. Clericus vel religiosus qui bona ad pias causas sive per actum inter vivos, sive ex testamento fiduciarie accepit, debet de sua fiducia Ordinarium certiorem reddere, eique omnia istiusmodi bona seu mobilia seu immobilia cum oneribus adiunctis indicare; quod si donator id expresse et omnino prohibuerit, fiduciam ne acceptet.

§ 2. Ordinarius debet exigere ut bona fiduciaria in tuto collocentur et vigilare pro exsecutione piae voluntatis ad normam can. 1515.

§ 3. Bonis fiduciariis alicui religioso commissis, si quidem bona sint attributa loci seu dioecesis ecclesiis, incolis aut piis causis iuvandis, Ordinarius de quo in §§ 1, 2, est loci Ordinarius; secus, est Ordinarius eiusdem religiosi proprius.

"The cleric or religious who has, either by way of donation or by last will, received goods in trust for pious causes, must notify the Ordinary concerning the trusteeship, and describe all such goods, both movable and immovable, with the obligations attached to them. If the donor has explicitly and absolutely forbidden all reference to the Ordinary in this manner, the cleric or religious shall not accept the trust. The Ordinary must demand that the goods received in trust be safely invested, and supervise the fulfillment of the pious intentions of the donor, as provided by Canon 1515. If a religious is put in trust of goods left in favor of any church of the place or of the diocese, or to help the residents or pious works of the diocese, the Ordinary spoken of in this Canon is the local Ordinary; otherwise, he is the Ordinary of the religious."[132]

Since the text of the canon is clear and self-explaining as far as the question here treated is concerned no further com-

---

Epitome, II, 583; Vromant, *De Bonis Ecclesiae Temporalibus*, p. 171; Woywod, *A Practical Commentary*, II, 175.

[132] Woywod, *A Practical Commentary*, II, 176.

ment is necessary. The reason this canon has been mentioned here is its close connection with canons 1515 and 1517.[133]

84. **Canon 1517:**

> **§ 1. Ultimarum voluntatum reductio, moderatio, commutatio, quae fieri ex iusta tantum et necessaria causa debent, Sedi Apostolicae reservantur, nisi fundator hanc potestatem etiam Ordinario loci expresse concesserit.**
>
> **§ 2. Si tamen executio onerum impositorum, imminutos reditus aliamve causam, nulla administratorum culpa, impossibilis evaserit, tunc Ordinarius quoque, auditis iis quorum interest, et servata, meliore quo fieri potest modo, fundatoris voluntate, poterit eadem onera aeque imminuere, excepta Missarum reductione quae semper Sedi Apostolicae unice competit.**

The reduction, moderation, and commutation of last wills, which should be done only for a just and necessary cause, is reserved to the Holy See, unless the one who made the will has expressly granted this power to the local ordinary. If, however, the fulfillment of the imposed obligations should become impossible in view of the diminution of the revenues or for some other cause apart from all blame of the administrators, then the ordinary as well, upon hearing all interested parties and observing as feasibly as he can the will of the founder, is enabled to effect an equitable reduction of the enjoined obligations, save those which attach to the celebration and application of Masses in relation to which the Holy See alone has competence.

---

[133] One may consult the following authors on this canon: Augustine, *Commentary*, VI, 574; Ayrinhac, *Administrative Legislation*, pp. 418-419; Blat, *De locis sacris et de bonis Ecclesiae temporalibus*, p. 583; Cocchi, *Commentarium*, VI, 380; Fanfani, *De Iure Religiosorum*, p. 196; Gerster a Zeil, *Ius Religiosorum*, p. 53; Nebreda, "Quaestiones Selectae,"—*CpRM*, VII (1926), 326; Schaefer, *De Religiosis*, p. 414; Vermeersch-Creusen, *Epitome*, II, 584.

Does the word *ordinary* in the second part of this canon refer exclusively to local ordinaries, or may it also refer to religious ordinaries? Augustine[134] and Woywod[135] say this canon refers exclusively to local ordinaries. In support of this view Woywod quotes the following from the Council of Trent: " 'In alterations of last wills—which alterations ought not to be made except for a just and necessary cause—the bishops, as delegates of the Apostolic See, shall, before the alterations aforesaid are carried into execution, ascertain that nothing has been stated in the prayer of the petition which suppressed what is true or suggests what is false.' "[136]

On the other hand, there are strong reasons for holding that religious ordinaries are also contemplated in this canon. First, there is the fact that the word *ordinary* is used without any modification. The second argument is taken from the fact that the reason why ordinaries have this power of changing wills in certain rare incidents is precisely because they are, according to canon 1515, the officially appointed executors of all last wills. Religious ordinaries enjoy this power equally with local ordinaries and consequently in those certain cases which are mentioned in canon 1517, § 2, they too are empowered to change last wills. This is the more probable as well as the more common opinion.[137]

The force of the above quotation from the Council of Trent can be offset by two other quotations from the same council, which give this power to religious ordinaries and are likewise noted in the Gasparri edition of the Code as sources of this second paragraph.[138] The text quoted by

---

[134] *Commentary,* VI, 576.

[135] *A Practical Commentary,* II, 177.

[136] Sess. XXII, *de ref.,* c. 6.

[137] Cf. Blat, *De locis sacris et de bonis Ecclesiae temporalibus,* p. 586: Cappello,*Summa Iuris Canonici,* II, 671 and III, 34; Coronata, *Institutiones,* II, 470; Gerster a Zeil, *Ius Religiosorum,* pp. 51-52; Hannan, *The Canon Law of Wills,* pp. 479-480.

[138] Sess. XXV, *de ref.,* c. 4: "Ubi nimius est Missarum faciendarum numerus, statuant Episcopi, Abbates et Generales Ordinum, quod expedire judicaverint." And sess. XXV, *de ref.,* c. 8: "Quod si hospi-

Woywod is cited in the Gasparri edition of the Code as a source only for paragraph one of canon 1517 which speaks explicitly of local ordinaries; consequently, it cannot be used as proof that paragraph two may not refer also to religious ordinaries. Paragraph two will refer to religious ordinaries in all cases in which they act as executors.

85. **Canon 1519, § 2:**

> **Habita ratione iurium, legitimarum consuetudinum et circumstantiarum, Ordinarii, opportune editis peculiaribus instructionibus intra fines iuris communis, universum administrationis bonorum ecclesiasticorum negotium ordinandum curent.**

Ordinaries should look to the careful management of all ecclesiastical goods under their jurisdiction. To this end they should issue special instructions at opportune times. The ordinary here referred to is the local ordinary as can be concluded from the context.[139] Religious ordinaries are

talia haec ad certum peregrinorum, aut infirmorum, aut aliarum personarum genus suscipiendum fuerint instituta, nec in loco, ubi sunt dicta hospitalia, similes personae, aut perpaucae reperiantur, mandat adhuc, ut fructus illorum in alium pium usum, qui eorum institutioni proximior sit, ac pro loco et tempore utilior, convertantur, prout Ordinario cum duobus de Capitulo, qui rerum usu peritiores sint, per ipsum deligendis, magis expedire visum fuerit; nisi aliter forte, etiam in hunc eventum, in eorum fundatione aut institutione fuerit expressum: quo casu, quod ordinatum fuit, observari curet Episcopus; aut, si id non possit, ipse, prout supra, utiliter provideat. Itaque ii praedicti omnes, et singuli, cujuscumque Ordinis, et religionis, et dignitatis, etiamsi laici fuerint, qui administrationem hospitalium habent, *non tamen regularibus subiecti, ubi viget regularis observantia*, ab Ordinario moniti hospitalitatis munus, adhibitis omnibus, ad quae tenentur, necessariis, re ipsa obire cessaverint, non solum per ecclesiasticas censuras, et alia iuris remedia ad id compelli possint, sed etiam hospitales ipsius administratione curave perpetuo privari possint, aliique eorum loco ab iis ad quos spectabit, substituantur." The italics are not in the original text.

[139] Cf. Ayrinhac, *Administrative Legislation*, p. 425; Cocchi, *Commentarium*, VI, 391; Voosen, "De Ordinarii Loci Vigilantia iuxta Can. 1519,"—*Ius Pontificium*, XV (1935), 273-279.

regulated regarding their rights and duties in this matter by a special chapter in the Code and by their own proper constitutions.[140]

Nevertheless, as Blat[141] very truly says, it is feasible and even expedient that also religious ordinaries should let themselves be guided by this prescription. In this connection it is good to recall that whatever the Code established as a general rule for all ecclesiastical administrators applies likewise to religious ordinaries unless the more specific legislation as contained in canons 531-537 and in their own constitutions provides otherwise.[142]

86. **Canon 1523:**

Administratores bonorum ecclesiasticorum diligentia boni patrisfamilias suum munus implere tenentur; ac proinde debent:

4° Pecuniam ecclesiae, quae de expensis supersit et utiliter collocari potest, de consensu Ordinarii, in emolumentum ipsius ecclesiae occupare.

Administrators shall, with the consent of the ordinary, invest for the good of their church all surplus revenues. According to the general principle stated above in n. 85, this canon will refer also to religious ordinaries.[143]

87. **Canon 1536, § 2:**

Donatio facta ecclesiae, ab eius rectore seu Superiore repudiari nequit sine licentia Ordinarii.

Any donation made to a church cannot be refused by the rector or superior of the same without permission of the

---

140 Canons 531-537.

141 *De locis sacris et de bonis Ecclesiae temporalibus*, p. 593.

142 Cf. Wernz-Vidal, *Ius Canonicum*, III, 173.

143 Thus Blat, *op. cit.*, p. 601; Pejska, *Ius Canonicum Religiosorum*, p. 69; Schaefer, *De Religiosis*, p. 417, note 42; Vromant, *De Bonis Ecclesiae Temporalibus*, p. 243. The individual constitutions of the various religions may incorporate the obligation here mentioned; cf. e.g., *Declarations and Constitutions of the Swiss-American Benedictine Congregation*, n. 56.

ordinary. In relation to churches belonging to an exempt clerical religion, this permission must be had from the major superior.[144]

88. Canon 1538:

> **§ 1. Si ecclesiae bona, legitima interveniente causa, oppignoranda vel hypothecae nomine obliganda sint, vel agatur de aere alieno contrahendo, legitimus Superior, qui ad normam can. 1532 licentiam dare debet, exigat ut antea omnes, quorum interest, audiantur, et curet ut, cum primum fieri poterit, aes alienum solvatur.**
> **§ 2. Hac de causa annuae ratae ab eodem Ordinario praefiniantur quae exstinguendo debito sint destinatae.**

"If the goods of a church are for a legitimate reason to be pledged or mortgaged, or debts are to be contracted, the legitimate superior who has according to Canon 1532 the right to grant permission shall insist that previously all parties interested are heard, and he shall see that debts are paid off as soon as possible. The same Ordinary shall for this purpose determine the annual rate at which the debt is to be extinguished."[145]

By analogy it can very well be said that the religious ordinary also should establish the annual rate at which debts should be paid off. This may be inferred, also, from the fact that when a religious house asks the Holy See for permission to contract more serious debts the Sacred Congregation of Religious demands that in the petition there be

---

[144] Thus Ayrinhac, *Administrative Legislation*, p. 450; Blat, *op. cit.*, p. 628; Cocchi, *Commentarium*, VI, 422; Gerster a Zeil, *Ius Religiosorum*, p. 52; Nebreda, "Quaestiones Selectae,—*CpRM*, VII (1926), 317, note 72; Vermeersch-Creusen, *Epitome*, II, 600; Vito, *Questioni Canoniche* (3 vols., Napoli, 1926-1929), III, 138; Wernz-Vidal, *Ius Canonicum*, IV, pars 2, 335; Woywod, *A Practical Commentary*, II, 187.

[145] Woywod, *A Practical Commentary*, II, 188.

expressed, among other things, a minute and accurate description of the means to be used in order to pay both the yearly interest and the debt itself.[146]

89. Canon 1539, § 2:

> **Administratores possunt *titulos ad latorem,* quos vocant, commutare in alios titulos magis aut saltem aeque tutos ac frugiferos, exclusa qualibet commercii vel negotiationis specie, ac de consensu Ordinarii, dioecesani Consilii administrationis, aliorumque quorum intersit.**

"Administrators may exchange notes payable to bearer for other valuable papers which are at least equally safe and profitable, but must avoid any kind of barter or trading; such transactions also require the consent of the Ordinary, the diocesan board of administration and other interested parties."[147]

Since this canon establishes a general statute prescribed for all administrators of church goods, and since it is not opposed to any of the prescriptions in canons 531-537, it can apply also to religious. In order to make such an exchange the administrator of the goods of an exempt clerical religion will need the consent of the religious ordinary and of his council, as well as any other interested party.[148] If the individual constitutions of the religious institute demand any other formalities, they must, of course, be complied with.

90. Canon 1541, § 2:

> **Pro locatione bonorum ecclesiasticorum, servato praescripto can. 1479:**

---

[146] Cf. the letter of the Apostolic Delegate at Washington issued on November 13, 1936, with the authority of the Sacred Congregation for Religious and sent to the moderators and to the woman superiors of the various religious communities.

[147] Woywod, *A Practical Commentary,* II, 189.

[148] Cf. Schaefer, *De Religiosis,* p. 428, note 107, and p. 430, note 114.

3° Si valor non excedat mille libellas seu francos et locatio sit ultra novennium, servari debet idem praescriptum can. 1532, § 2; si locatio non sit ultra novennium, fieri potest a legitimis administratoribus, monito Ordinario.

In leasing ecclesiastical goods, if the lease does not extend over nine years and does not exceed one thousand francs,[149] it may be made by the legitimate administrator, who must inform the ordinary of the fact. Since the temporal administration of goods belonging to religious is governed by canon 543, this present canon can be applied only indirectly to religious, i.e., in so far as this canon accurately determines what leases are to be governed by the rules for the alienation of property. Any lease for a time longer than nine years is to be considered an alienation and must be governed accordingly.[150]

D. Commentary on Book IV

91. The ordinary ecclesiastical judicial processes are governed by the canons of Book IV. Canon 1555, § 1, states that the Holy Office has its own proper method of procedure which must be observed. In paragraph three of this same canon exception is made for the process which is necessary before a religious with perpetual vows can be dismissed from a clerical exempt institution. All other tribunals, whether diocesan or religious,[1] must be governed by the canons in this book of the Code unless, by a special privilege

[149] About $200.00, or rather, according to the present value of the dollar, about $340.00. Cf. Doheny, "Church Finance and Problems of Alienation,"—*The Jurist,* I (1941), 102.

[150] Cf. Vermeersch-Creusen, *Epitome,* II, 604; Cocchi, *Commentarium,* VI, 428; and Blat, *De locis sacris et de bonis Ecclesiae temporalibus,* p. 635.

[1] Cf. Lega-Bartoccetti, *Commentarius in Iudicia Ecclesiastica iuxta Codicem Iuris Canonici* (2 vols., Romae: Anonima Libraria Cattolica Italiana, 1938-1939), I, 94.

or by a special disposition of the legislator, they are permitted or obliged to use different norms.[2]

Although the holding of trials is an affair alien to the general concept of what befits a religious house, nevertheless judicial action must be considered in so far as it affects clerical exempt communities. The need for a special tribunal for exempt religious is a result of the following facts: 1.) First, *latae sententiae* penalties, unless the fact that they have been incurred is notorious, do not have their full effect before a declaratory sentence is passed concerning them.[3] Although, according to canon 2223, § 4, the declaration of such a penalty is generally left to the good judgment of the superior, yet it must be effected if an interested party or the common good requires it.

2.) Secondly, concerning *ferendae sententiae* penalties, the superior must obey the law and inflict the penalty unless the law itself permits otherwise. The law, indeed, permits the superior under certain conditions to defer the application of the penalty to a more opportune time or to moderate it and in certain cases even to abstain from inflicting it altogether.[4] Moreover, some penalties can be inflicted by a particular precept without any process at all.[5] With the exception of these cases, however, all penalties for public crimes must be inflicted only after due process of law.[6]

3.) Thirdly, the court for settling all controversies between religious of the same exempt clerical organization is the court of the provincial superior or of the local abbot for autonomous monasteries, unless the individual constitutions provide otherwise.[7]

---

[2] Cf. Noval, *De Iudiciis* (Augustae Taurinorum—Romae: 1920), p. 29.

[3] Cf. canon 2232, § 1.

[4] Cf. canon 2223, nn. 1-3.

[5] Cf. canon 1933, § 4.

[6] Cf. Pejska, *Ius Canonicum Religiosorum*, p. 244.

[7] Cf. canon 1579, § 1; cf. also Roberti, *De Processibus* (2. ed., Romae: Apud Custodiam Librariam Pontificii Instituti Utriusque Iuris, 1940), pp. 209-210-211.

For these general reasons exempt religious have had their own tribunal distinct from that of the place in which they reside ever since the year 1245, when Innocent IV in the I General Council of Lyons decreed that they were not held to answer in the tribunals of the local ordinaries except in certain cases.[8] The Code has acknowledged this tradition and has made it even more precise and clear, as it has also done in the legislation for diocesan courts. Both tribunals are ruled by the same laws. These canons concerning processes, however, are applicable to religious tribunals only in so far as the competence of these tribunals is extended.

In view of all that has thus far been said, it can be held that the present Code treats religious tribunals as *ordinary* tribunals and legislates for them accordingly in the same canons which concern diocesan tribunals.[9] On the other hand, as Roberti[10] likewise holds, religious tribunals are more correctly called special tribunals, since they are based on the privilege of exemption and since their competence is limited by that exemption. For this reason and also because of the small number of cases treated, religious institutions do not as a rule have permanently established courts for the trying of all cases. Whenever the need arises, a special court is constituted.[11] This is another point in which they differ from diocesan courts, for the latter must be permanently constituted in each diocese.[12] If these few preliminary remarks are kept in mind, the following comments will be more easily understood and appreciated.

92. Canon 1562:

§ 1. Qui peregrinus est in Urbe, licet per breve tempus, potest in ipsa tanquam in proprio domicilio citari; sed ius habet revocandi domum, idest petendi ut ad proprium Ordinarium remittatur.

---

[8] C. 1, *de privilegiis*, V, 7, in VI°.

[9] Cf. Roberti, *De Processibus*, p. 98.

[10] *De Processibus*, p. 426; also p. 210.

[11] Cf. Roberti, *De Processibus*, p. 248.

[12] Cf. canons 1572, 1573, 1574, 1578, 1586, etc.

§ 2. Qui in Urbe ab anno commoratur, ius habet declinandi forum Ordinarii et instandi ut coram Urbis tribunalibus citetur.

Any Catholic visiting Rome, even though only for a short time, can be cited before the Roman tribunal just as he can be cited before the court of his own domicile, although he has the right to ask that he be tried before his own ordinary. If one has lived in Rome for one year, he has the right of refusing to appear before the court of his own ordinary and of demanding that he be tried at Rome. Just as citizens of the old Roman Empire were considered in the law as citizens of the city of Rome itself, so also now all Christians are considered in a certain sense as having a common domicile at Rome, where the common father of all Christians resides.[13] Since the Code acknowledges this privilege for all Christians who happen to be in Rome, it holds also for religious.[14] The opinion of Blat[15] which holds that this privilege cannot be invoked by religious seems untenable. Their privilege of exemption from the local ordinary does not exclude them from enjoying the privilege of this canon which is common to *all* Christians. The text of the canon itself makes no restriction as to the application of this privilege. It can be invoked with perfect right, therefore, by any Catholic, wether he be a layman or a member of the diocesan or of the regular clergy, provided only that he be a "peregrinus in Urbe" as the canon says.

---

[13] Cf. c. 20, X, *de foro competenti,* II, 2; cf. also the *Acts of the Apostles,* XXV, 10. Very expressive of the fact that the Roman church is the first church of all Christendom is the inscription on the front of the church of St. John Lateran in Rome: "Sacrosancta Lateranensis Ecclesia Omnium Urbis et Orbis Ecclesiarum Mater et Caput."

[14] Cf. Cappello, *Summa Iuris Canonici,* III, 80.

[15] *De Processibus* (Romae: Apud Institutum Pontificium Internationale "Angelicum," 1927), pp. 23-25.

93. Canon 1580:

§ 1. Potest Ordinarius unum aut plures auditores, seu actorum instructores, sive stabiliter sive pro certa aliqua causa constituere.

§ 2. Iudex auditorem eligere potest tantummodo pro causa quam cognoscit, nisi Ordinarius iam providerit.

The ordinary can appoint one or several auditors either permanently or for any individual case. A judge can appoint an auditor for the case which he tries unless the ordinary has already provided one.

From the fact that canon 1581 prescribes that in religious tribunals the auditor must be a member of the same religious institute, it follows that his election will depend on the religious ordinary. This is the common opinion of the authors,[16] and is amply confirmed by the various readings this canon underwent before it became crystallized in its final form in the Code.[17] Thus *schemata B* and *C* refer to "Episcopus"; *schemata D, E,* and *F* have "Potest loci Ordinarius"; but *schema G* and the Code have "Potest Ordinarius."

94. Canon 1585, § 2:

Quare iudex, antequam causam cognoscere incipiat, in actuarium assumere debet unum e notariis legitime constitutis, nisi ipse Ordinarius aliquem pro ea causa iam designaverit.

The judge before trying a case must choose one of the legitimately constituted notaries as secretary, unless the

---

[16] Cf. Blat, *De Processibus*, p. 54; Coronata, *Institutiones*, III, 32; Lega-Bartoccetti, *Commentarius*, I, 142; Noval, *De Iudiciis*, p. 72; Pejska, *Ius Canonicum Religiosorum*, p. 245.

[17] Cf. Roberti, *Codicis Iuris Canonici Schemata*, Lib. IV, *De Processibus*, I, *De Iudiciis in Genere* (Civitas Vaticana: Typis Polyglottis Vaticanis, 1940), pp. 52-53. This work will be quoted hereafter simply as *Schemata* together with the page to which reference is made.

ordinary has already designated one for that case. In the tribunals of religious the religious ordinary may designate this official for a special case if he so desires, as is clear from the fact that religious tribunals, as also all religious discipline, exist in dependence on the religious superior.[18] Canon 503, moreover, explicitly states that religious ordinaries can officially appoint notaries for affairs pertaining to their jurisdiction. It may be added also that *schemata D* and *E* of the Code use the word "Episcopus" here, while *schemata F, G,* and the Code use simply the word "Ordinarius."[19]

95. Canon 1586:

> **Constituatur in dioecesi *promotor iustitiae* et *defensor vinculi*: ille pro causis, tum contentiosis in quibus bonum publicum, Ordinarii iudicio, in discrimen vocare potest, tum criminalibus; iste pro causis, in quibus agitur de vinculo sacrae ordinationis aut matrimonii.**

In every diocese a promoter of justice and a defender of the bond must be constituted; the first for criminal cases and contentious cases in which, according to the judgment of the ordinary, the public welfare is concerned; the latter in cases in which is called in question the validity either of sacred ordination or of matrimony. From the context, "in dioecesi," it is seen that the word *ordinary* in this canon refers directly only to local ordinaries. Moreover, the Code here provides for the appointment of a permanent holder for these offices. In exempt clerical institutions a promoter of justice generally is not appointed except for a particular

---

18 Cf. Roberti, *De Processibus*, p. 246.

19 Roberti, *Schemata*, pp. 58-59; cf. also Cappello, *Summa Iuris Canonici*, III, 95; Cocchi, *Commentarium*, VII, 54; Lega-Bartoccetti, *Commentarius*, I, 149; Noval, *De Iudiciis*, p. 81; Pejska, *Ius Canonicum Religiosorum*, p. 245; Schaefer, *De Religiosis*, p. 781; Wernz-Vidal, *Ius Canonicum*, VI, 93.

case.[20] Furthermore, the Code speaks of the election of a defender of the bond for cases of matrimony and sacred orders. In neither of these two cases has the religious ordinary any jurisdiction. Nevertheless, by way of analogy, this canon can be applied to religious ordinaries, in so far as they also have the right and duty to nominate a promoter of justice when the need arises, as shall be declared in the following n. 96.

96. Canon 1589, § 1:

> **Ordinarii est promotorem iustitiae et vinculi defensorem eligere, qui sint sacerdotes integrae famae, in iure canonico doctores vel ceteroqui periti, ac prudentiae et iustitiae zelo probati.**

It is the duty of the ordinary to elect as promoter of justice and as defender of the bond priests who are known for their integrity, who have a doctorate, or who are at least well versed in canon law, and who are likewise recognized for their prudence and for their love of justice. In the religious tribunal the promoter of justice must be, moreover, a member of the same religious organization. From the second paragraph of this canon it is clear that a promoter of justice is sometimes at least needed also in a religious tribunal. In such a case, since the entire trial pertains to the religious ordinary, so also will it pertain to him to choose the promoter of justice.[21] The various *schemata* of the Code confirm this reasoning in that *schemata A, B,* and *C* speak of the "Episcopus," while *schemata D, E, F, G,* and the Code use the broader term "Ordinarius." Moreover, *F, G,* and the Code add the second paragraph, which expressly pertains to religious tribunals.[22]

---

[20] Cf. Coronata, *Institutiones,* III, 37, note 6; and Roberti, *De Processibus,* p. 416.

[21] Cf. Coronata, *Institutiones,* III, 37, note 6; Pejska, *Ius Canonicum Religiosorum,* p. 245; and Roberti, *De Processibus,* p. 341.

[22] Roberti, *Schemata,* pp. 64-65.

There can be no trial before a religious tribunal in which a defender of the bond need be named; hence it is never in the religious ordinary's power to elect such an official. It is true that in the process concerning the nullity of a religious profession, Benedict XIV[23] had decreed that there should be a defender of the validity of the religious profession who was to function very much in the same way as the defender of the bond in matrimonial cases. This official, however, was dropped from these processes even before the Code, for there is no mention of him in the rules for these processes issued by the Sacred Congregation for Religious on May 16, 1911.[24] For this reason one cannot agree with Lega-Bartoccetti in their statement that: "Constituendus est promotor iustitiae seu defensor professionis religiosae in religione clericali exempta pro causa dimissionis professi a votis perpetuis, ex can. 655, § 2 et can. 1589, § 2."[25] In the footnote of the Gasparri edition of the Code the Constitution *"Si datam"* of Benedict XIV is not given as a source for canon 655, § 2, but reference is made only to the above mentioned instruction. This evidently indicates that the promoter of justice who must be elected according to that canon is not to be at the same time the defender of the validity of the religious profession as prescribed by Benedict XIV. Moreover, in this special trial for the dismissal of religious it is not the religious ordinary who elects this promoter of justice, but the supreme moderator himself as the canon clearly states.

97. Canon 1599, § 1: Sacra Rota iudicat:

1° In secunda instantia causas quae a quorumvis Ordinariorum tribunalibus in primo gradu diiudicatae fuerint et ad Sanctam Sedem per appelationem legitimam deferantur.

---

[23] Const. *"Si datam,"* 4 mart. 1748, § 11—*Fontes*, n. 385.

[24] Cf. *Fontes*, n. 4409; Blat (*De Processibus*, p. 61) and Noval (*De Iudiciis*, p. 80) expressly state that this defender as a special official no longer exists.

[25] *Commentarius*, I, 156.

The Sacred Rota tries in the second instance all cases which have been tried in the first instance in the courts of any of the ordinaries and have been referred to the Holy See by legitimate appeal. Since the Code speaks indiscriminately of cases tried before *all* ordinaries, and since there is nothing to the contrary in the canons that relate specifically to religious, the cases tried before religious ordinaries will also go before the Sacred Rota, if they are appealed to Rome.[26]

98. Canon 1601:

Contra Ordinariorum decreta non datur appellatio seu recursus ad Sacram Rotam; sed de eiusmodi recursibus exclusive cognoscunt Sacrae Congregationes.

No appeal or recourse can be had to the Sacred Rota from the decrees of any ordinary. The reason is the following: *decrees* are issued administratively and therefore any redress which is sought against them must be obtained from an administrative body, e.g., from one of the Sacred Congregations, and not from a judicial one, e.g., from the Sacred Rota. Since the decrees of religious ordinaries are classified in this same administrative category, redress against them can not be obtained from the Sacred Rota, but only from the proper Sacred Congregation.[27]

99. Canon 1614, § 2:

Si ipsemet Ordinarius sit iudex et contra ipsum exceptio suspicionis opponatur, vel abstineat a iudicando vel quaestionem suspicionis definiendam committat iudici immediate superiori.

If the ordinary himself acts as judge in a case and the exception of suspicion is lodged against him, he should

[26] Thus Blat, *De Processibus*, p. 75; Lega-Bartoccetti, *Commentarius*, I, 171; Noval, *De Iudiciis*, p. 100; Roberti, *De Processibus*, pp. 227-237.

[27] Cf. Blat, *De Processibus*, p. 77.

either refrain from trying the case personally or refer the exception to the next superior for an authoritative decision. This regulation clearly refers also to the religious ordinary for the following reasons: 1.) The word *ordinary* is used by itself and hence it must be understood according to canon 198, § 1; 2.) The canon lays down a general prescription for *all* processes; consequently religious tribunals must also conform to it;[28] 3.) *Schema C* of the Code has for this canon "loci Ordinarius," but *schema G* and the Code use the more inclusive term "Ordinarius," thus indicating that religious ordinaries are also meant.[29]

100. Canon 1615:

§ 2. Ordinarii autem est in locum iudicum qui suspecti declarati sunt, alios a suspicione immunes subrogare.

§ 3. Quod si ipsemet Ordinarius declaratus fuerit suspectus, idem peragat iudex immediate superior.

In the place of any judge who is declared suspect the ordinary will appoint another who is free from suspicion. If, however, even the appointing ordinary is declared suspect, the new judge or judges will be appointed by the next higher superior. For the same three reasons as those given with relation to the preceding canon, the present canon also must be regarded as referring to religious ordinaries.[30]

101. Canon 1621, § 1:

Excepto Episcopo qui per se potestatem iudiciariam exerceat, omnes qui tribunal constituunt aut eidem opem ferunt, iusiurandum de officio rite et

---

[28] Cf. Blat, *De Processibus*, p. 99; Coronata, *Institutiones*, III, 55; Lega-Bartoccetti, *Commentarius*, I, 226; Noval, *De Judiciis*, p. 119.

[29] Roberti, *Schemata*, pp. 100-101.

[30] Cf. Blat, *De Processibus*, p. 101; Roberti, *De Processibus*, 246; *idem*, *Schemata*, p. 103; *schema E* has "Ordinarii autem loci est"; *schemata F* and *G* and the Code, however, have "Ordinarii autem est"; paragraph three of canon 1615 has no precedents in the various *schemata*.

fideliter implendo coram Ordinario vel coram iudice a quo electi sunt, vel coram viro ecclesiastico ab alterutro delegato, praestare debent: idque ab initio suscepti officii, si sint stabiles, aut antequam causa agatur, si pro peculiari aliqua causa sint constituti.

"Except the bishop when he sits in person as judge, all persons who constitute or assist a tribunal must take an oath before the Ordinary or the judge by whom they are chosen, or before an ecclesiastic delegated either by the Ordinary or the judge, that they will fulfill their office properly and faithfully. The oath is to be taken at the beginning of their office, if they are regular officials, or before the beginning of the trial, if they were appointed for one particular case only."[31]

Again the same three reasons as those which were given in n. 99 are applicable. This fact argues that the word *ordinary* as here used refers also to the religious ordinaries.[32]

102. **Canon 1648, § 3:**

Sed in causis spiritualibus et cum spiritualibus connexis, si minores usum rationis assecuti sint, agere et respondere queunt sine patris vel tutoris consensu; et quidem, si aetatem quatuordecim annorum expleverint, etiam per seipsos, secus per tutorem ab Ordinario datum, vel etiam per procuratorem a se, Ordinarii auctoritate, constitutum.

"In spiritual cases or in cases connected with spiritual affairs, minors who have attained the use of reason can sue and defend without the consent of the parent or tutor; if

---

[31] Woywood, *A Practical Commentary*, II, 218.

[32] Cf. Biederlack-Führich, *De Religiosis*, p. 68; Noval, *De Judiciis*, p. 126; Roberti, *De Processibus*, p. 452; *idem*, *Schemata*, pp. 104-105; *schema C* has "coram Episcopo"; *schemata D* and *E* have "coram loci Ordinarii"; but *schemata F*, *G*, and the Code have simply "coram Ordinario."

they are fourteen years of age, they can in person plead their case, but otherwise they must plead through a tutor appointed by the Ordinary, or by a tutor chosen by the minor with the approval of the Ordinary."[33]

Most authors do not consider the question of the possible reference which in this canon is implied relative also to religious ordinaries. Augustine, however, very justly considers it worthy of note that "the apposition 'loci' is omitted, and hence, according to can. 198, the superiors of clerical exempt institutes are also competent" to appoint or approve the guardian as determined in this canon.[34] But it must also be noted that before this canon can refer to a religious ordinary there must be question of a minor who is subject to him (in any one of the ways mentioned in canon 514, § 1) and also of a case in which the religious tribunal is competent. Ordinarily, however, one or both of the parties in such a controversy will be of the diocesan clergy, or of the laity, and consequently the local ordinary will be exclusively competent.

103. Canon 1649:

> **Nomine eorum de quibus in can. 100, § 3, stat in iudicio rector vel administrator, firmo praescripto can. 1653; in conflictu vero eorum iurium cum iuribus rectoris vel administratoris, procurator ab Ordinario designatus.**

In trials moral persons are represented by their rectors or administrators, except in the cases mentioned in canon 1653; if, however, their rights are in conflict with the rights of the rector or administrator, the ordinary shall designate a special procurator for the moral person. Blat[35] is of the opinion that the word *ordinary* here refers exclusively to the local ordinary. As proof of this he adduces canon 1519 which states: "Loci Ordinarii est sedulo advigilare adminis-

[33] Woywod, *A Practical Commentary,* II, 229.

[34] *Commentary,* VII, 101.

[35] *De Processibus,* p. 148.

trationi omnium bonorum ecclesiasticorum quae in suo territorio sint nec ex eius iurisdictione fuerint subducta..." This very canon, however, can be cited as proving that the local ordinary has no authority over the temporal goods of clerical exempt institutes, for such goods have been exempted from subjection to his jurisdiction. The administration of these goods will pertain to the religious ordinary. Through the application of this principle to the present canon the following result is established: For moral persons which are wholly subject to a religious ordinary, this latter will be the proper ordinary to designate a procurator. For all other moral persons, the proper ordinary will be the local ordinary.[36]

104. Canon 1651:

> **§ 1. Ut curator ab auctoritate civilii alicui datus a iudice ecclesiastico admittatur, debet accedere consensus Ordinarii proprii illius cui datus est.**
> **§ 2. Ordinarius potest quoque alium curatorum constituere pro foro ecclesiastico, si, omnibus mature perpensis, id statuendum esse prudenter censuerit.**

Before a guardian who is appointed by the civil authorities for anyone can be admitted in an ecclesiastical court, he must have the consent of the proper ordinary of his ward. The ordinary can also, if he judges it prudent, appoint another guardian for the ecclesiastical court. From the very wording of the canon there can be no doubt as to the ordinary to whom reference is here made. The canon reads: "debet accedere consensus Ordinarii proprii illius cui datus [curator] est." Therefore, if such a guardian is constituted for any person who is a subject of the religious ordinary, this latter must give his consent before the guardian can be admitted into an ecclesiastical court; otherwise the local ordinary must give the consent.[37]

---

[36] Cf. Augustine, *Commentary*, VII, 101.

[37] Cf. Augustine, *Commentary*, VII, 101.

105. Canon 1658:

§ 1. Quilibet pro lubitu a parte potest eligi et deputari procurator, dummodo secundum praecedentem canonem idoneus sit, quin opus sit ut Ordinarii approbatio antecesserit.

§ 2. Advocatus autem, ut ad patrocinium admittatur, indiget approbatione Ordinarii, quae aut generalis sit ad omnes causas aut specialis pro certa causa.

Anyone having the required qualities according to canon 1657 may be chosen as a proxy without the previous approval of the ordinary. However, a person may not be permitted to act as advocate in a case without the approval of the ordinary. With regard to this canon arguments which are akin to the three proposed in n. 99 above can be used to show that religious ordinaries are also comprised under the term *ordinary* in these two paragraphs.[38] It is, of course, recognized that for a diocesan tribunal the local ordinary alone, and not the religious ordinary, is competent. For cases, however, which are tried before the religious tribunal, the approval of the major superior is sufficient for one to act as advocate in the trial.[39]

It may perhaps be objected that paragraph one cannot refer to religious ordinaries since it demands that a proxy must have the qualities which are demanded in canon 1657, which requires in its paragraph three that a religious cannot act as proxy or advocate except with the permission of the superior. Paragraph one, however, of canon 1658 is not contrary to that, because it merely says that this per-

---

[38] Cf. *supra*, n. 99, pp. 122-123; also Roberti, *Schemata*, pp. 150-151; *schemata C*, *D*, and *E* have "ab Ordinario loci"; *schemata F* and *G* and the Code, however, in changing the order of the words, leave out the word "loci" and read as follows: "quin opus sit ut Ordinarii approbatio antecesserit."

[39] Cf. Blat, *De Processibus*, p. 166; and Pejska, *Ius Canonicum Religiosorum*, p. 246.

mission or approval does not necessarily have to precede the deputation of anyone in the capacity of proxy.

106. Canon 1813, § 1:

> **Praecipua documenta publica ecclesiastica haec sunt:**
>
> **1° Acta Summi Pontificis et Curiae Romanae et Ordinariorum in exercitio suorum munerum authentica forma exarata, itemque attestationes authenticae de iisdem actibus datae ab illis vel eorum notariis;**
>
> **4° Inscriptiones baptismi, confirmationis, ordinationis, professionis religiosae, matrimonii, mortis, quae habentur in regestis Curiae vel paroeciae, vel religionis, et attestationes scriptae ex iisdem desumptae et a parochis, vel Ordinariis, vel notariis ecclesiasticis confectae aut earum exemplaria authentica.**

The principal public ecclesiastical documents are: 1.) Authentically composed acts of the Holy Father, of the Roman Curia and of ordinaries in the exercise of their duties; also authentic attestations of these acts given by one of the above authorities or by a lawful notary . . . 4.) "records of baptism, confirmation, ordination, religious profession, marriage, and death, which are preserved in the Curia, or the parish, or the religious organization; also written attestations taken from the said records made by pastors, or Ordinaries, or ecclesiastical notaries, and authentic copies of them."[40] The Code establishes the rule that all documents of public acts drawn up and signed by one who exercises ordinary authority must be given public credence. Those, however, who do not exercise ordinary, or at least duly delegated, jurisdiction must have recourse to a public notary in the drawing up of public documents.[41]

[40] Woywod, *A Practical Commentary,* II, 284.

[41] Cf. Lega-Bartoccetti, *Commentarius,* II, 784, note 1.

Religious ordinaries, since they exercise ordinary jurisdiction, are, therefore, included under the term *ordinary* as used in this canon. Moreover, from the very context it is evident that religious ordinaries are also referred to, for the canon speaks among other things of "inscriptiones... professionis religiosae ... quae habentur in regestis ... religionis."[42]

107. Canon 1939, § 1:

> **Si delictum nec notorium sit nec omnino certum, sed innotuerit sive ex rumore et publica fama, sive ex denuntiatione, sive ex querela damni, sive ex inquisitione generali ab Ordinario facta, sive alia quavis ratione, antequam quis citetur ad respondendum de delicto, inquisitio specialis est praemittenda ut constet an et quo fundamento innitatur imputatio.**

"If an offense is neither notorious nor altogether certain, but has become known through rumor and public report, or through denunciation, or from complaint for damages, or from general inquiry instituted by the Ordinary, or from any other cause, a special investigation must be conducted to ascertain whether and how far the incrimination is justified, before a person can be summoned to answer for his offense."[43]

Since the Code here uses the word *ordinary* by itself and since there is question here of a matter which could occur in a religious institute to religious, there is reference in this canon to the religious ordinary also. The general inquiry or inquisition referred to is the ordinary visitation which all ordinaries and superiors must make at certain stated times.[44] That this canon and the following ones, which con-

---

[42] Cf. Blat, *De Processibus,* pp. 328-329; Coronata, *Institutiones,* III, 246-247; Noval, *De Iudiciis,* p. 368.

[43] Woywood, *A Practical Commentary,* II, 328.

[44] Cf. Blat, *De Processibus,* p. 462; Pejska, *Ius Canonicum Religiosorum,* p. 246.

cern the judicial investigation, should be applied at least sometimes by religious superiors when they make such an investigation is clear likewise from the express declaration of canon 658 which, when it speaks of the investigation that is to be made before the dismissal of a religious, demands explicitly that the prescriptions of canons 1939-1946 be observed in the carrying out of the investigation.

108. Canons 1942, § 1 and 1946, §§ 1 and 2 and § 2, n. 2:

These two canons lay down various rules with regard to the conducting of the special inquisition or investigation which has been mentioned in the preceding number. Whenever there is question of the conducting of such an investigation of the actions of a religious member of a clerical exempt institute the proper ordinary to begin and to carry through the procedure will be the major superior.[45]

109. Canons 1947; 1948, n. 3; 1950; 1951, § 2:

These canons deal with the judicial rebuke which the ordinary may employ in place of a criminal process whenever the accused person confesses his guilt and there is question of a case in which this substitution is not forbidden by the canons. Granted the authority of religious ordinaries with regard to the judicial trials of their subjects, these canons will most certainly refer also to the religious ordinary in those same cases.[46]

110. Canon 1994, § 1:

> **Validitatem sacrae ordinationis accusare valet clericus peraeque ac Ordinarius cui clericus subsit vel in cuius dioecesi ordinatus sit.**

---

[45] Cf. Blat, *De Processibus*, pp. 466 and 469; Gerster a Zeil, *Ius Religiosorum*, p. 157; Mayer, *Ordensrecht*, IV, 125; Schaefer, *De Religiosis*, pp. 785 and 1015; and Pejska, *Ius Canonicum Religiosorum*, p. 246.

[46] Cf. Blat, *De Processibus*, pp. 472-474; Coronata, *Institutiones*, III, 400; Noval, *De Iudiciis*, p. 523; Pejska, *Ius Canonicum Religiosorum*, p. 246.

"The right to attack the validity of sacred ordination rests equally with the cleric and the Ordinary to whom the cleric is subject, or in whose diocese he was ordained."[47]

The canon itself is clear, since it gives this right to the ordinary "cui clericus subsit," i.e., also to the religious ordinary for his own subjects; nevertheless it is not unwarranted to declare explicitly that the religious ordinary has this right with regard to the ordination of any of the clerics subject to him.[48]

111. Canon 2144, § 2; 2145, §1; and 2146, § 3:

Since all these special cases treated in canons 2142-2194 refer primarily and principally to the diocesan clergy and the local ordinary, it is only natural that the legislator should make provision in these canons especially for them. Nevertheless titles XXXI[49] and XXXIII[50] can refer also to religious simply in their capacity as religious, as will be explained later on. Consequently, when the word *ordinary* is used without modification in these two processes, it will refer likewise to the major superiors of exempt clerical religious. The same must be said of the introductory canons which enact general rules to be observed in all the subsequent cases. Therefore, in the canons now under consideration, 2144, 2145, and 2146, religious ordinaries are also referred to. That statement, however, must be understood with due regard for their condition as religious, e.g., in canon 2145, § 1, one finds: "auditis parochis consultoribus seu examinatoribus." That would seem to exclude religious ordinaries. But if it is considered that these introductory canons give the norms to be followed for all the summary processes, and if it is admitted, as will be proved further

[47] Woywood, *A Practical Commentary,* II, 350.

[48] Cf. Blat, *De Processibus,* p. 531; Cappello, *Summa Iuris Canonici,* III, 355; Cocchi, *Commentarium,* VII, 502; Coronata, *Institutiones,* III, 440.

[49] *De modo procedendi contra clericos concubinarios.*

[50] *De modo procedendi in suspensione ex informata conscientia infligenda.*

on, that titles XXXI and XXXIII furnish applicable norms for religious ordinaries as well as for local ordinaries, then all of these introductory canons must be interpreted in such a way as not to exclude the competence of religious ordinaries in cognate matters that come under their jurisdiction.[51]

112. Canons 2176-2180:

These canons deal with the process: "De modo procedendi contra clericos concubinarios." This process is applicable also for religious, as is evident, or at least hinted at in canon 2359, § 1, which says that all clerics in sacred orders, whether belonging to the secular or to the *religious* clergy, who are delinquent in this point should be punished according to the prescripts of canons 2176-2181. Perhaps it will be objected that this process is not necessary for religious, since they are always "amovibilis ad nutum." But removal from the parochial office is not the only thing in question here. These canons declare in a preceptive, and not merely in a directive way, just what punishments should be inflicted on such delinquents, whether they be religious or diocesan priests.[52] The first use of the word *ordinarius* in

[51] Coronata (*Institutiones*, III, 541) says that in matters in which the local ordinary must ask the advice of his examiners or consultors the religious ordinary must ask the advice of his council.

[52] Coronata, *Institutiones*, III, 541 and 542: "Religiosos in sacris in religione clericali exempta iudicat Ordinarius religiosus. Tribunal constituitur Ordinario, Actuario, examinatoribus synobalibus, et pro Ordinario religioso, suo Consilio loco examinatorum."...."Si agitur de clerico non beneficiato aut de religioso, unicum remedium applicabile est suspensio a divinis." Emmanuel Suarez (*De Remotione Parochorum aliisque processibus tertiae Partis Lib. IV Cod. Iur. Can.* [Romae: Apud Pontificium Internationale Institutum "Angelicum" de Urbe, 1931], 156-157) holds the same opinion: "Cum etiam his sanctionibus poenalibus subiiciantur clerici religiosi, ut constat ex verbis can. 2359, § 1, sub numero praecedentis relatis, in religionibus clericalibus exemptis pro suis subditis, potest has sanctiones iniungere Superior Maior, cum ipse veniat quoque nomine Ordinarii."

canon 2180 can refer also to religious ordinaries, but the second can refer only to the local ordinary, for the question is one of his jurisdiction over a cleric who holds a benefice as its irremovable incumbent. For the same reason canon 2181 cannot refer to a religious ordinary.

113. Canons 2186-2194:

These canons regulate the manner in which ordinaries are to procede in the suspension of clerics *ex informata conscientia* as it is called. Although the Code does not explicitly state that *religious* ordinaries can inflict this penalty, nevertheless there is no doubt that they also, in the same way as local ordinaries, have this power over their own clerical subjects with respect to such jurisdictional acts in which the major superior is given full and exclusive exercise and control.[53]

E. COMMENTARY ON BOOK V

114. Canon 2237:

> **§ 1. In casibus publicis potest Ordinarius poenas latae sententiae iure communi statutas remittere, exceptis:**
>
> **1° Casibus ad forum contentiosum deductis;**

[53] Cf. Augustine, *Commentary,* VII, 473; Blat, *De Processibus,* p. 704; Cocchi, *Commentarium,* VII, 648; ; Coronata, *Institutiones,* III, 556; Nicola Fanelli, *La Procedura Canonica nei Processi Amministrativi et Penali* (Vicenza: Società Anonima Tipografica fra Cattolici Vicentini, 1936), pp. 96-97; Gerster a Zeil, *Ius Religiosorum,* p. 254; Murphy, *Suspension Ex Informata Conscientia* (The Catholic University of America, Canon Law Studies, n. 76, Washington, D. C.: The Catholic University of America, 1932), pp. 49 and 114; Noval, *De Iudiciis,* p. 386 and p. 410; Pejska, *Ius Canonicum Religiosorum,* p. 247; Schaefer, *De Religiosis,* p. 350; Suarez, *De Remotione Parochorum,* pp. 215-216; Vermeersch-Creusen, *Epitome,* III, 210; Wernz-Vidal, *Ius Canonicum,* VI, 762; and Woywod, *A Practical Commentary,* II, 400; *idem,* "Procedural Law of the Code,"—*Homiletic and Pastoral Review,* XXXV (1935), 1286.

2° Censuris Sedi Apostolicae reservatis;

3° Poenis inhabilitatis ad beneficia, officia, dignitates, munera in Ecclesia, vocem activam et passivam eorumve privationis, suspensionis perpetuae, infamiae iuris, privationis iuris patronatus et privilegii seu gratiae a Sede Apostolica concessae.

§ 2. In casibus vero occultis, firmo praescripto can. 2254 et 2290, potest Ordinarius poenas latae sententiae iure communi statutas per se vel per alium remittere, exceptis censuris specialissimo vel speciali modo Sedi Apostolicae reservatis.

In public cases the ordinary can remit all *latae sententiae* penalties established by the common law except those mentioned in nn. 1, 2, and 3 of paragraph one of canon 2237. In occult cases, without prejudice to canons 2254 and 2290, the ordinary can remit all *latae sententiae* penalties except those which are reserved in a special or in a very special way to the Holy See. Since, with regard to their own subjects, the major superiors of exempt clerical religions have practically the same jurisdiction as bishops with regard to their subjects, they also can remit all the penalties mentioned in this canon, provided that the delinquent is subject to their authority.[1] As is evident, much greater authority

---

[1] Cf. Augustine, *Commentary,* VIII, 110; Ayrinhac, *Penal Legislation in the New Code of Canon Law* (revised edition, New York: Benziger, 1936), p. 52; Claeys Bouuart-Simenon, *Manuale,* I, 135; Cappello, *Summa Iuris Canonici,* III, 410; Cerato, *Censurae Vigentes ipso facto a Codice iuris canonici excerptae* (2. ed., Patavii, 1921), p. 39; Cocchi, *Commentarium,* VIII, 86; Coronata, *Institutiones,* IV, 134 and 139; Fanfani, *De Iure Religiosorum,* pp. 72-73; Mayer, *Ordensrecht,* II, 190; Michiels, *Normae Generales,* II, 480; Pejska, *Ius Canonicum Religiosorum,* p. 237; Pellé, *Le Droit Pénal de L'Eglise* (Paris: P. Lethielleux, 10 Rue Cassette, 1939), p. 70; Roberti, *De Delictis et Poenis* (Romae: Apud Custodiam Librariam Pontificii Instituti Utriusque Iuris, Vol. I, Pars I, (n. d.); Vol. I, Pars II, 1938), Vol. I, Pars II, 305-306; Salucci, *Il Diritto Penale Secondo Il Codice di Diritto Canonico* (2 vols., Subiaco, I, 1926; II, 1930), I, 167; Schaefer, *De Religiosis,* pp. 235-236; Smith, *The Penal Law for Religious*

is given to the ordinary to remit penalties in occult cases than in public cases. What Cappello[2] says in reference to the absolution from censures is applicable also to this canon which treats of the remission of penalties, namely, that relative to this absolution or remission all those who are enumerated in canon 514, § 1, are to be considered as subjects of the religious ordinary, just as they also are considered his subjects with regard to confessional jurisdiction according to canon 875, § 1. He, as well as the local ordinary, can delegate the jurisdiction necessary for the hearing of their confessions.

115. Canons 2301 and 2302:

Canon 2301: Ordinarius nequit praescribere ut clericus certo in loco, extra fines suae dioecesis, commoretur, nisi accedat consensus Ordinarii illius loci vel agatur de domo poenitentiae seu emendationis clericis non solum dioecesanis, sed etiam extraneis destinata, aut de domo religiosa exempta, Superiore eiusdem consentiente.

Canon 2302: Tam praescriptio quam prohibitio certo in loco commorandi et collocatio in domo poenitentiae aut in domo religiosa, praesertim si diu duraturae sint, imponantur tantum in casibus gravibus, in quibus, prudenti Ordinarii iudicio, eae poenae necessariae sint ad clerici emendationem aut scandali reparationem.

The ordinary cannot command that a cleric should reside in a particular place outside of his own diocese except with

(The Catholic University of America, Canon Law Studies, n. 98, Washington, D. C.: The Catholic University of America 1935), p. 130; Vermeersch-Creusen, *Epitome*, I, 168 and III, 254; Wernz-Vidal, *Ius Canonicum*, I, 471 and VII, 222; Woywod, *A Practical Commentary*, II, 425; Blat, *De Delictis et Poenis* (Romae: Apud Institutum Pontificium Internationale "Angelicum," 1924), p. 85.

[2] *Summa Iuris Canonici*, III, 407 and *Tractatus Canonico-Moralis de Censuris iuxta Codicem Iuris Canonici* (3. ed., Taurinorum Augustae—Romae: Marietti, 1933), p. 117.

the permission of the ordinary of that place or unless there is question of a house of correction or penance for all clerics, or of an exempt religious house. In this last case the superior's permission must be had. If one judges from the text alone, then it seems that this canon refers only to local ordinaries.[3] The canon states "extra fines suae dioecesis," thus implying a direct reference to local jurisdiction and consequently to local ordinaries. However, by the use of legitimate analogy this canon is seen to have reference likewise to religious ordinaries.[4]

Good order demands that, if a religious superior should have to punish one of his subjects by commanding residence in some place other than in a house subject to that superior, then the consent of the local ordinary of that place should be obtained. If, however, the house to which the subject is sent is under the jurisdiction of a religious ordinary, then the consent of that religious ordinary must be had. In this case there will be no obligation to obtain the consent of the local ordinary of the place in which the religious house to which the subject is sent is situated.

What has been said concerning canon 2301 must be applied likewise to canon 2302. The individual constitutions of the various religious organizations must, of course, be followed if they prescribe anything with regard to this type of punishment.

116. Canons 2303-2304:

These two canons deal with the very severe punishments of deposition, perpetual privation of the ecclesiastical garb, and degradation. Since religious are ruled by canons 646-672 whenever there is need for the infliction of a severe punishment, the word *ordinary* in the canons here considered refers exclusively to local ordinaries.[5] According

---

[3] Blat, *De Delictis et Poenis*, p. 184.

[4] Cf. Cocchi, *Commentarium*, VIII, 199.

[5] Cf. Mayer, *Ordensrecht*, II, 182; and Schaefer, *De Religiosis*, pp. 1023-1026.

to canons 646-672, dismissal from the religious community is the most severe punishment inflicted within the religion. This punishment can not be inflicted by the religious ordinary himself, but only by the supreme moderator together with his council. Any further punishment is inflicted either *ipso iure* or by the proper local ordinary.[7]

117. Canon 2321:

Sacerdotes qui contra praescripta can. 806, § 1, 808 praesumpserint Missam eodem die iterare vel eam celebrare non ieiunii, suspendantur a Missae celebratione ad tempus ab Ordinario secundum diversa rerum adiuncta praefiniendum.

Priests who, contrary to canons 806 and 808, presume to celebrate Mass twice on the same day or to celebrate Mass after they have broken their fast shall be suspended from the celebration of Mass for a time to be determined by the ordinary according to the various circumstances. Although religious ordinaries cannot grant permission for bination, nevertheless, if one of their subjects binates without the required permission either from the Holy See or from the local ordinary, the religious ordinaries are competent to punish the offender.[8]

118. Canon 2329:

Ecclesiae vel coemeterii violatores, de quibus in can. 1172, 1207, interdicto ab ingressu ecclesiae aliisque congruis poenis ab Ordinario pro gravitate delicti puniantur.

Those who violate a church or cemetery in any of the ways recounted in canons 1172 and 1207 shall be punished by the ordinary with an interdict from entering the church

[6] Cf. canons 669, § 2; 670; and 671, nn. 1 and 3.

[7] Cf. canon 671, nn. 4 and 6.

[8] Cf. Blat, *De Delictis et Poenis*, p. 211; Coronata, *Institutiones*, IV, 320; and Salucci, *Il Diritto Penale*, II, 52.

and with other suitable penalties in line with the gravity of the crime committed. Although canon 2269, which gives to bishops the power of inflicting both local and personal interdicts, does not refer to religious ordinaries, nevertheless these latter enjoy the same right in that they can inflict a personal interdict on their own subjects.[9] Their jurisdiction is personal. Therefore they have no authority either by law or by custom to inflict a local interdict which of its very nature would affect also those who are not subject to the religious ordinary.

Against this common opinion of the authors Roberti[10] has advanced a new opinion which denies religious ordinaries the faculty of inflicting even a personal interdict. He argues that religious superiors have lost this power through custom which has been confirmed in canon 2269, § 1, of the Code, which states that some interdicts can be declared only by the Holy See while others can be inflicted by the *bishops*. His argument is that the Code in this canon uses the word *bishops* and not *ordinaries* expressly in order to exclude religious ordinaries.

This opinion is certainly not without weight. Nevertheless it hardly seems a strong enough argument to disavow for religious ordinaries the jurisdiction to inflict personal interdicts on their own subjects, which power they did have, as is attested by all the above cited authors. The celebrated commentator, Wernz,[11] writing in 1913, states that custom has indeed restricted the rights of religious ordinaries with regard to local interdicts but not with regard to personal

---

[9] Cf. Augustine, *Commentary*, VIII, 199; Beste, *Introductio in Codicem*, p. 921; Blat, *De Delictis et Poenis*, p. 218; Cappello, *De Censuris*, p. 407; Conran, *The Interdict* (The Catholic University of America, Canon Law Studies, n. 56, Washington, D. C.: The Catholic University of America, 1930), pp. 60-61; Wernz-Vidal, *Ius Canonicum*, VII, 311.

[10] *De Delictis et Poenis*, Vol. I, Pars II, 426.

[11] *Ius Decretalium*, VI, 229, note 497: "Quae potestas Praelatorum regularium saltem ex consuetudine recepta restricta est ad ius infligendi interdictum *personale*, non vero locale."

interdicts. This doctrine is amply corroborated by the particular laws of the various religious institutes as evidenced in their constitutions which even now have force of law and which give to the religious ordinary the faculty of inflicting the censure of a personal interdict.[12]

119. Canon 2337:

§ 1. Si parochus, ad impediendum exercitium ecclesiasticae iurisdictionis, ausus fuerit turbas ciere, publicas pro se subscriptiones promovere, populum sermonibus aut scriptis excitare aliaque similia agere, pro gravitate culpae, secundum prudens Ordinarii iudicium, puniatur, non exclusa, si res ferat, suspensione.

§ 2. Eodem modo puniat Ordinarius sacerdotem qui multitudinem quoquo modo excitet ad impediendum ingressum in paroeciam sacerdotis legitime nominati in parochum aut oeconomum.

"If, for the purpose of hindering the exercise of ecclesiastical jurisdiction, a pastor shall dare to stir up the populace, to promote public subscriptions in his favor, to stir up the people by speeches or writings, or to take other similar actions, he shall be punished at the discretion of the ordinary with penalties proportioned to his guilt, and, if necessary, even with suspension. In the same manner the Ordinary shall punish a priest who excites the multitude in any manner to prevent a priest who has been legitimately nominated as pastor or administrator from entering a parish."[13]

---

[12] Cf. *Declarations and Constitutions of the Swiss-American Congregation, O. S. B.*, p. 19: "Each abbot, and also the abbot praeses of the Congregation, since they are ecclesiastical judges, can, by observing the proper procedure, inflict censures of excommunication, of suspension, and of interdict with all the effects of law upon those subject to their jurisdiction."

[13] Woywood, *A Practical Commentary*, II, 486-487.

Although there is here question of a matter affecting diocesan discipline and, consequently, of a matter in which even exempt religious are subject to the local ordinary, yet the competence of the religious ordinary over his own subjects is by no means altogether excluded. In fact, as was pointed out in the first part of this thesis, canon 631, § 2, explicitly states that an exempt religious who fails against his duties as a parish priest can be punished by both the local and the religious ordinary.[14]

120. Canon 2342:

> **Plectuntur ipso facto excommunicatione Sedi Apostolicae simpliciter reservatae:**
>
> **1° Clausuram monialium violantes, cuiuscumque generis aut conditionis vel sexus sint, in earum monasteria sine legitima licentia ingrediendo, pariterque eos introducentes vel admittentes; quod si clerici sint, praeterea suspendantur per tempus pro gravitate culpae ab Ordinario definiendum.**

"Excommunication simply reserved to the Apostolic See is automatically incurred . . . by persons of whatever class, condition or sex who violate the enclosure of nuns by entering their monasteries without legitimate permission, and also by persons who introduce or admit them. If they are clerics, they shall, moreover, be suspended for a period of time to be fixed by the Ordinary in proportion to the gravity of their guilt."[15]

Local ordinaries according to a tradition confirmed by canons 512, § 2, n. 1, and 601, § 2, are the officially appointed guardians of the observance of the enclosure of nuns. Therefore, they have the authority and the duty of seeing that all those who break this enclosure, even if they be exempt religious, are duly punished.[16] For their own

---

[14] Cf. Blat, *De Delictis et Poenis*, p. 226; and Cocchi, *Commentarium*, VIII, 271.

[15] Woywod, *A Practical Commentary*, II, 493.

[16] Cf. Salucci, *Il Diritto Penale*, II, 161.

subjects religious ordinaries also are competent to inflict the suspension prescribed by canon 2342, for the canon uses the term *ordinary* without any modification whatever.[17]

121. Canon 2347:

Firma nullitate actus et obligatione, etiam per censuram urgenda, restituendi bona illegitime acquisita ac reparandi damna forte illata, qui bona ecclesiastica alienare praesumpserit aut in iis alienandis consensum praebere contra praescripta can. 534, § 1, et can. 1532:

2° Si agatur de re cuius pretium sit supra mille, sed infra triginta millia libellarum, privetur patronus iure patronatus; administrator munere administratoris; Superior vel oeconomus religiosus, proprio officio et habilitate ad cetera officia, praeter alias congruas poenas a Superioribus infligendas; Ordinarius vero aliique clerici, officium, beneficium, dignitatem, munus in Ecclesia obtinentes, solvant duplum favore ecclesiae vel piae causae laesae; ceteri clerici suspendantur ad tempus ab Ordinario definiendum.

"In addition to the nullity of the act and the obligation —which is to be enforced even with censures—to make restitution of the goods unlawfully acquired and the duty to repair the damages which may have been caused, a person who presumes to alienate ecclesiastical goods or gives his consent thereto in violation of the precepts of Canons 534 and 1532, shall be punished as follows: .... (2) if the goods have a value of over one thousand and less than thirty thousand francs, a patron who is guilty of illegal alienation shall be deprived of the right of patronage; an administrator of his office of administration; a religious Superior or religious *oeconomus* of his office and of eligibility to acquire any other office, in addition to other appropriate penalties

[17] Cf. Blat. *De Delictis et Poenis,* p. 235.

to be imposed by the Superiors; an Ordinary and other clerics who hold an office, benefice, dignity, or position in the Church, shall pay double the amount to the church or pious institute which has been injured; other clerics shall be suspended for a length of time to be determined by the Ordinary."[18]

In the last two phrases of n. 2 of this canon the word *ordinary* is used without any modification so that it would seem to refer also to religious ordinaries. However, since the canon devotes a special phrase to religious: "a religious Superior or religious *oeconomus* shall be deprived of his office and of eligibility to acquire any other office, in addition to other appropriate penalties to be imposed by the Superiors," the last two phrases concerning which there is question here are clearly designated for local ordinaries and the diocesan clergy.[19] Moreover, the canon treats of a punishment and, therefore, the time-honored aphorism: *Odiosa sunt restringenda,* must be applied to the exclusion of the religious ordinaries.

122. Canon 2373:

> **In suspensionem per annum ab ordinum collatione Sedi Apostolicae reservatam ipso facto incurrunt:**
>
> **1° Qui contra praescriptum can. 955, alienum subditum sine Ordinarii proprii litteris dimissoriis ordinaverint.**

Suspension for a year from the conferring of orders is automatically incurred by him who, against the prescription of canon 955, ordains a subject of another ordinary without the dimissorial letters of the proper ordinary. Since canon 964, n. 2, declares that no bishop can licitly ordain an exempt religious without dimissorial letters from the proper major superior, the question arises: Does a

---

[18] Woywod, *A Practical Commentary,* II, 497-498.

[19] Cf. Blat, *De Delictis et Poenis,* p. 245; and Coronata, *Institutiones,* IV, 455.

bishop who ordains an exempt religious of his own diocese without the proper dimissorials incur the suspension named in canon 2373, n. 1? There is no doubt that the ordination would be undertaken illicitly. The bishop, however, would not incur the suspension mentioned here, because, according to the strict wording of the canon, only he who confers orders *contrary to the demands of canon* 955 will incur the punishment. Canon 955, however, does not contain any reference to religious.

For this reason it seems incorrect to comment on this canon as Ayrinhac does: "The suspension . . . is incurred by . . . the prelate who ordains, without dimissorial letters, a candidate who is not his subject."[20] According to that wording bishops who confer orders contrary to the demands of canon 964, n. 2, would also be suspended from conferring orders for a year. There is question here of a punishment and therefore, according to canon 19, the strict interpretation must be followed. Consequently, the word *ordinary* in n. 1 of canon 2373 does not refer to religious ordinaries but exclusively to local ordinaries.

---

[20] *Penal Legislation,* p. 284.

GENERAL CONCLUSION

Now that the Code has been considered in its entirety, one realizes better the full meaning of canon 198, § 1, in so far as it refers to religious. One realizes that the juridical presumption does in fact militate for religious ordinaries. This presumption, however, has certain limitations established by law. As has been seen, these limitations are numerous. Not only has canon 198, § 1, the limiting clauses: "pro suis vero subditis" and "nisi quis expresse excipiatur," but canon 615 also indicates definite exceptions as enacted by law, even though it establishes the general rule of exemption for all regulars. This exemption is limited by the clause: "praeterquam in casibus a iure expressis." Therefore, to understand the juridical figure which is signalized by the term *religious ordinary,* one must not only understand the fundamental principle that all major superiors of exempt clerical religions are ordinaries, but one must also understand what limitations are placed on this fundamental principle and why. To obtain such an understanding has been the purpose of this thesis.

In the comments on the individual canons an effort has been made to avoid exaggerating or minimizing the true meaning and extent of the privilege of exemption as it is applied and understood in the Code. Since the rights and duties of local and of religious ordinaries at times overlap, at least in so far as both exercise jurisdiction in certain matters over the same subjects, it is useful to recall what has been written before the Code on the subject of the interrelation and necessary unity that should exist between the apostolic labors of the diocesan and of the religious clergy. In order to exemplify this pre-Code outlook the writer takes the liberty of quoting two passages from pre-Code legislative sources. The first of these is excerpted from the Constitution *Romanos Pontifices* of Pope Leo XIII:[1] "Religious,

[1] May 8, 1881, § 27: "Sic enim fiet, ut Episcoporum ductu et prudentia religiosi sodales de Anglicis missionibus apprime meriti, strenue

whose merit in the English missions is certainly very great, should zealously and eagerly continue to reap the gratifying fruits of their apostolic labors under the prudent guidance of the bishops and *both,* to use the words of St. Gregory the Great to the bishops of England, *with oneness of mind and action should with a Christian emulation determine what must be done, and, having carefully considered matters, should carry out their right judgments without any disagreement.* Such cooperation is demanded by the paternal care of bishops for their helpers and the corresponding filial devotedness of clerics towards their bishops; the end for which all must strive with oneness of thought and action—the salvation of souls—demands it; the necessity of resisting those who are hostile to Catholicism also demands it. This cooperation begets power and makes even the weak equal to the greatest tasks; it is a sign that distinguishes the true disciples of Christ from those who belie their calling. In view of all this we exhort you one and all to this concord in the Lord, begging with Paul that you bring this joy to our hearts, namely, that you be of one mind, of one heart, and of one soul."[2]

---

et alacriter e laboribus suis fructus salutis ferre pergant laetissimos, atque utrique (ut voce utamur Gregorii Magni ad Angliae Episcopos) *communi . . . consilio, concordique actione quae sunt pro Christi zelo agenda disponant unanimiter, recte sentiant, et quae senserint, non sibimet discrepando perficiant.* Concordiam hanc postulat paterna caritas Episcoporum in adiutores suos et mutua Cleri in Episcopos observantia; hanc concordiam flagitat finis communis qui situs est in salute animarum iunctis studiis ac viribus quaerenda; hanc eamdem exigit necessitas iis resistendi qui catholico nomine infensi sunt. Haec vires gignit et infirmos quoque pares efficit ad grandia quaeque gerenda; haec signum est quod sinceros Christi discipulos ab iis disterminat qui se tales esse mentiuntur. Ad hanc igitur singulos et universos enixe cohortamur in Domino, rogantes cum Paulo ut impleant gaudium Nostrum, ut idem sapiant eamdem caritatem habentes, unanimes, idipsum sentientes."—*Fontes,* n. 582; cf. also paragraph 7 of this same constitution.

[2] For this translation and for the translation of the following text from the *Corpus Iuris Canonici* the writer wishes to express his thanks to his confrere, Father Conrad Louis, O. S. B.

The second passage is taken from the *Corpus Iuris Canonici*:[3] "Since the Church is one and the same for all whether they be prelates or subjects, members of the diocesan or of the regular clergy, exempt or nonexempt, and since no one is saved outside of that one Church in which all have the same Lord, the same faith, and the same baptism, it is only fitting that all, who are thus members of the same one body, should be likewise of the same will, brethren, joined together by the bonds of fraternal charity. Let all, therefore, prelates as well as subjects, exempt and nonexempt, be content with their rights."[4]

---

[3] C. un., *de excessibus praelatorum*, V, 6, in Clem.: "Verum quia una est regularium et secularium praelatorum et subditorum exemptorum et non exemptorum universalis Ecclesia, extra quam nullus omnino salvatur, quorum omnium unus est Dominus, una fides, et unum baptisma: decet ut omnes qui eiusdem sunt corporis, unius etiam sint voluntatis; et sicut fratres ad invicem vinculo charitatis sint adstricti. Decet igitur ut et praelati et alii, tam exempti quam non exempti suis iuribus sint contenti."

[4] Cf. *supra*, note 2; and also the encyclical letter *"Ubi primum,"* of June 17, 1847, addressed to all the moderators of religious orders, found in *Pii IX Pontificis Maximi Acta, Pars Prima* (Romae, 1854), I, 46-54. Cf. also the letter *"Venerabilis Frater,"* of June 17, 1847, sent to all local ordinaries together with the above mentioned encyclical *"Ubi primum,"* found in the same work as before cited, I, 55-56.

PARTICULAR CONCLUSIONS

1. Before the Code major superiors of exempt clerical religions had with but a few exceptions the same jurisdiction over their own subjects that local ordinaries had over their diocesans.

2. The Code has not changed the legislation with regard to major superiors of exempt clerical religions, but has confirmed it and made it more precise in canon 198, § 1.

3. The religious ordinary has jurisdiction only with regard to his own subjects, among whom must be numbered in certain matters all those who are named in canon 514, § 1.

4. With regard to judicial processes religious ordinaries must observe the same regulations and laws as local ordinaries, *mutatis mutandis*.

5. The same penal legislation in the Code that governs the exercise of a local ordinary's jurisdiction governs likewise the exercise of jurisdiction by the religious ordinary.

BIBLIOGRAPHY

Sources

Acta Apostolicae Sedis, Commentarium Officiale, Romae, 1909—

Acta et Decreta Sacrorum Conciliorum Recentiorum, Collectio Lacensis, 7 vols., Friburgi Brisgoviae, 1870-1890.

Bullarum Diplomatum et Privilegiorum Sanctorum Romanorum Pontificum, Taurinensis editio, 24 vols. et Appendix, Augustae Taurinorum-Neapoli, 1857-1872.

Canones et Decreta Sacrosancti Oecumenici Concilii Tridentini, Romae, 1882.

Codex Iuris Canonici Pii X Pontificis Maximi iussu digestus Benedicti XV autoritate promulgatus, Romae: Typis Polyglottis Vaticanis, 1917.

Codicis Iuris Canonici Fontes cura Emi. Petri Card. Gasparri Editi, 9 vols., Romae (postea Civitate Vaticana): Typis Polyglottis Vaticanis, 1923-1938. (Vols. VII-IX *ed. cura et studio Emi. Iustiniani Card. Serédi.*)

Collectanea S. Congregationis de Propaganda Fide, 2 vols., Romae, 1907.

Corpus Iuris Canonici, ed. Lipsiensis 2., Aemilius Ludovicus Richter-Aemilius Friedberg, ed., anastatice repetita, 2 vols., Lipsiae: Tauchnitz, 1928.

Corpus Iuris Civilis (Kreuger-Mommsen-Scholl-Kroel), 5. ed., 3 vols., Berolini, 1928-1929.

Declarations and Constitutions of the Swiss-American Benedictine Congregation, Conception Abbey, Conception, Mo.: Altar and Home Press, 1938.

Decreta Authentica Congregationis Sacrorum Rituum, 6 vols., Romae, 1898-1927.

Reference Works

Aertnys, Josephus, et Damen, Cornelius, *Theologia Moralis secundum Doctrinam S. Alfonsi de Ligorio*, 2 vols., 13. ed., Taurini: Marietti, 1939.

Ayrinhac, H. A., *Administrative Legislation in the New Code of Canon Law*, New York: Longmans, 1930.

———, *General Legislation in the New Code of Canon Law*, New York: Longmans, 1933.

———, *Legislation on the Sacraments in the New Code of Canon Law*, New York: Longmans, 1928.

———, and Lydon, P. J., *Penal Legislation in the New Code of Canon Law*, revised edition, New York: Benziger, 1936.

[Bachofen], Charles Augustine, *A Commentary on the New Code of Canon Law*, St. Louis: Herder, Vol. I, 6. ed., 1931; Vol. II, 6. ed., 1936; Vol. III, 5. ed., 1938; Vol. IV, 3 ed., 1925; Vol. V, 5. ed., 1935; Vols. VI and VIII, 3. ed., 1931; Vol. VII, 3. ed., 1930.

———, *Rights and Duties of Ordinaries*, St. Louis: Herder, 1924.

Badii, Caesar, *Institutiones Iuris Canonici*, 2. ed., 2 vols., Florentiae, 1922.

Barbosa, Augustinus, *De Officio et Protestate Episcopi*, Lugduni, 1628.

Benedictus XIV, *Institutiones Ecclesiasticae*, Romae, 1747.

———, *De Synodo Diocesana*, 3 vols., Romae, 1783.

Berutti, Chr., *Institutiones Iuris Canonici*, 3 vols., Taurini: Marietti, 1936.

Beste, Udalricus, *Introductio in Codicem*, Collegeville, Minn.: St. John's Abbey Press, 1938.

Biederlack, Ios.,—Führich, Max., *De Religiosis*, Oeniponte, 1919.

Blat, Albertus, *Normae Generales*, Romae: Apud Institutum Pontificium Internationale "Angelicum," 1921.

———, *De Personis*, 1921.

———, *De Religiosis et Laicis*, 3. ed., 1938.

———, *De Sacramentis*, 1924.

———, *De Locis Sacris et de Bonis Ecclesiae Temporalibus*, 2. ed., 1934.

———, *De Processibus*, 1927.

———, *De Delictis et Poenis*, 1924.

Bliley, Nicholas M., *Altars according to the Code of Canon Law*, The Catholic University of America, Canon Law Studies, n. 38, Washington, D. C.: The Catholic University of America, 1927.

Bondini, A., *De Privilegio Exemptionis*, Romae, 1919.

Bouscaren, T. L., *Canon Law Digest*, 2 vols. and 2 supplements, Milwaukee: Bruce, 1934-1941.

Brunini, Joseph B., *The Clerical Obligations of Canons 139 and 142*, The Catholic University of America, Canon Law Studies, n. 103, Washington, D. C.: The Catholic University of America, 1937.

Cance, A., *Le Code de Droit Canonique*, 3 vols., Paris, 1927-1929.

Cappello, Felix M., *Tractatus Canonico-Moralis de Sacramentis*, 3 vols. in 6, Taurinorum Augustae: Marietti, Vol. I, 3. ed., 1938; Vol. II, pars I, 3. ed., 1938; Vol. II, pars II, 1932; Vol. II, pars III, 1935; Vol. III, partes I-II, 4. ed., 1939.

———, *Summa iuris Canonici*, 3 vols., Romae: Apud Aedes Universitatis Gregorianae, Vols. I-II, 3. ed., 1938-1939; Vol. III, 1936.

———, *Tractatus Canonico-Moralis De Censuris iuxta Codicem Iuris Canonici*, 3. ed., Taurinorum Augustae—Romae: Marietti, 1933.

Cerato, Prosdocimus, *Censurae Vigentes ipso facto a Codice iuris canonici excerptae,* 2. ed., Patavii, 1921.

Chelodi, Ioannes, *Ius de Personis,* 2. ed., a Sac. Ernesto Bertagnolli recognita et aucta, Tridenti : Libr. Edit. Tridentum, 1927.

Cicognani, Amleto Giovanni, *Canon Law,* Authorized English Version by J. O'Hara and F. Brennan, 2. ed., Philadelphia: The Dolphin Press, 1935.

Claeys Bouuaret, F.—Simenon, G., *Manuale Iuris Canonici,* 3 vols., Gandae et Leodii: Prostat apud Auctores in Seminariis Gandavensi et Leodiensi, 1934.

Cocchi, Guidus, *Commentarium in Codicem Iuris Canonici,* 8 vols., Taurinorum Augustae: Marietti, Vol. I, 5. ed., 1938; Vol. II, 4. ed., 1937; Vol. III, 3. ed., 1931; Vols. IV-V, 3. ed., 1932; Vol. VI, 3. ed., 1933; Vol. VIII, 3. ed., 1940; Vol. VIII, 4. ed., 1938.

Coronata, Matthaeus Conte a, *Institutiones Iuris Canonici,* 5 vols., Romae: Marietti, Vols. I-II, 2. ed., 1939; Vol. III, 1933; Vol. IV, 1935; Vol. V, 1936.

———, *De Locis et Temporibus Sacris,* Augustae Taurinorum: Marietti, 1922.

Creusen, Joseph-Garesché, Edward F.-Ellis, Adam C., *Religious Men and Women in the Code,* 3. English ed., Milwaukee: Bruce, 1940.

Dictionnaire de Droit Canonique, fasc. I-XV, Paris, 1928-1939.

Dictionnaire de Théologie Catholique, Vacant-Mangenot-Amann, XIV vols., Paris, 1903-1939.

Eichmann, E., *Lehrbuch des Kirchenrechts,* 2. ed., Paderborn, 1926.

Fanfani, L., *De Iure Religiosorum ad normam Codicis Iuris Canonici,* 2. ed., *Augustae Taurinorum,* 1925.

Ferrari, Joseph C., *Summa Institutionum Canonicarum,* 3. ed., 2 vols., Januae, 1877.

Ferraris, F. Lucius, *Prompta Bibliotheca, Canonica, Juridica, Moralis, Theologica necnon Ascetica, Polemica, Rubricistica, Historica,* ed. Migne, 8 vols., Parisiis, 1860-1863.

Gerster a Zeil, Thomas, *Ius Religiosorum,* Taurini: Marietti, 1935.

Goyeneche, S., *Iuris Canonici Summa Principia seu Breves Codicis Iuris Canonici Commentarii Scholis Accommodati, Partes II et III, Libri II,* Romae: Tip. Pol. "Cuore di Maria," 1938.

Guilfoyle, M. J., *Custom,* The Catholic University of America, Canon Law Studies, n. 105, Washington, D. C.: The Catholic University of America, 1937.

Hannan, Jerome, *The Canon Law of Wills,* The Catholic University of America, Canon Law Studies, n. 86, Washington, D. C.: The Catholic University of America, 1934.

Jansen, J., *Ordensrecht*, 3. ed., Paderborn: Verlag Ferdinand Schöningh, 1931.

Lega, M.-Bartoccetti, V., *Commentarius in Iudicia Ecclesiastica iuxta Codicem Iuris Canonici*, 2 vols., Romae: Anonima Libraria Cattolica Italiana, 1938-1939.

Lehmkuhl, Augustinus, *Theologia Moralis*, 12. ed., 2 vols., Friburgi Brisgoviae, 1914.

Maroto, Ph., *Institutiones Iuris Canonici ad Normam Novi Codicis*, 2 vols., Romae, Vol. I, 3. ed., 1921; Vol. II, 1919.

Mayer, H. Suso, *Benediktinisches Ordensrecht in der Beuroner Kongregation*, 4 vols., Hohenzollern: Kunstverlag Beuron, 1929-1936.

Michiels, Gommarus, *Normae Generales Juris Canonici*, 2 vols., Lublin: Universitas Catholica, 1929.

Molitor, R., *Religiosi Iuris Capita Selecta*, Ratisbonae, 1909.

Mothon, J. P., *Institutions Canoniques*, 3 vols., Paris, 1922.

———, *Traité sur L'État Religieux*, Paris, 1922.

Mühlbauer, Wolfgang, *Decreta Authentica Congregationis Rituum*, 4 vols., Monachii, 1865-1867.

Noldin, H.-Schmitt, A., *Summa Theologiae Moralis iuxta Codicem Iuris Canonici*, 24. ed., 3 vols., Oeniponte: F. Rauch, 1936.

Noval, Joseph, *De Iudiciis, Augustae* Taurinorum-Romae: Marietti, 1920.

———, *De Modo Procedendi in Nonnullis Expediendis Negotiis vel Sanctionibus Poenalibus Applicandis*, 1932.

Oesterle, Gerardus, *Praelectiones Iuris Canonici*, Romae: Apud Collegium S. Anselmi, 1931.

Ojetti, B., *Commentarium in Codicem Iuris Canonici*, 4 vols., Romae: Apud Aedes Universitatis Gregorianae, 1927-1931.

Papi, H., *Religious in Church Law*, New York, 1924.

Pejska, Josephus, *Ius Canonicum Religiosorum*, 3. ed., Friburgi Brisgoviae: Herder, 1927.

Pellé, P., *Le Droit Pénal de L'Église*, Paris: P. Lethielleux, 10 Rue Cassette, 1939.

Pernicone, Joseph M., *The Ecclesiastical Prohibition of Books*, The Catholic University of America, Canon Law Studies, n. 72, Washington, D. C.: The Catholic University of America, 1932.

Pistocchi, Marius, *De Re Beneficiali Iuxta Canones*, Taurini, 1928.

Raus, J. B., *Institutiones Canonicae*, 2. ed., Paris: Typis Emmanuelis Vitte, 1931.

———, *De Sacrae Obedientiae Virtute et Voto*, Lugduni, 1923.

Reilly, Edward M., *The General Norms of Dispensation*, The Catholic University of America, Canon Law Studies, n. 119, Washington, D. C.: The Catholic University of America Press, 1939.

Roberti, F., *De Processibus,* 2. ed., Romae: Apud Custodiam Librariam Pontificii Instituti Utriusque Iuris, 1940.

———, *De Delictis et Poenis,* Romae: Apud Custodiam Librariam Pontificii Instituti Utriusque Iuris, Vol. I, Pars I, (n. d.); Vol. I, Pars II, 1938.

———, *Codicis Iuris Canonici Schemata, Lib. IV, De Processibus, I, De Iudiciis in Genere,* Civitate Vaticana: Typis Polyglottis Vaticanis, 1940.

Roelker, Edward G., *Principles of Privilege according to the Code of Canon Law,* The Catholic University of America, n. 35, Washington, D. C.: The Catholic University of America, 1926.

Salucci, Raffaele, *Il Diritto Penale secondo Il Codice di Diritto Canonico,* 2 vols., Subiaco, I, 1926; II, 1930.

Sartori, Cosmas, *Enchiridion Canonicum,* Vicetiae: Ex typographia Commerciali, 1938.

Schaefer, Timotheus, *De Religiosis,* 3. ed., Rome: Herder, 1940.

Segatori, D. R., *Lo Stato Religioso,* Torino, 1923.

Sipos, Stephanus, *Enchiridion Iuris Canonici,*, 3. ed., Pécs: Ex Typographia "Haladás R. T.", 1936.

Smith, M. T., *The Penal Law for Religious,* The Catholic University of America, Canon Law Studies, n. 98, Washington, D. C.: The Catholic University of America, 1935.

Stadtmüller, Raphael Maria, *Das neue Ordensrecht,* Dülmen, 1919.

Suarez, Emmanuele, *De Remotione Parochorum Aliisque Processibus Tertiae Partis Lib. IV Cod. Iur. Can.,* Romae; Apud Pontificium Internationale Institutum "Angelicum" de Urbe, 1931.

Toso, Albertus, *Ad Codicem Iuris Canonici Commentaria Minora,* 5 vols., Romae: Marietti, 1920-1934.

Van Hove, A., *De Legibus Ecclesiasticis,* Mechliniae—Romae: H. Dessain, 1930.

———, *De Consuetudinis et Temporis Supputatione,* Mechliniae—Romae: H. Dessain, 1933.

———, *De Rescriptis,* Mechliniae—Romae: H. Dessain, 1936.

———, *De Privilegiis,* Mechliniae—Romae; H. Dessain, 1939.

Vermeersch, A.,-Creusen, J., *Epitome Iuris Canonici,* 3 vols., Mechliniae: H. Dessain, Vol. I, 6. ed., 1937; Vol. II, 5. ed., 1934; Vol. III, 5. ed., 1936.

Vito, Pasquale, *Questioni Canoniche,* 3 vols., Napoli, 1926-1929.

Vromant, G., *De Bonis Ecclesiae Temporalibus ad usum utriusque cleri praesertim Missionariorum et religiosorum,* Louvain, 1927.

Wernz, Franciscus X., *Ius Decretalium ad Usum Praelectionum in Scholis Textus Canonici sive Iuris Decretalium,* 6 toms. in 10 vols., Prati, Tom. I, 3. ed., 1913; Tom. III, pars. 1, 2, 3. ed., 1915; Tom. III, pars. 1, 2, 2. ed. (Romae), 1908; Tom. IV, pars. 1, 2, 2. ed., 1911-1912; Tom. V, pars. 1, 2, 1914; Tom. VI, 1914.

Wernz, F.-Vidal, P., *Ius Canonicum,* 7 toms. in 8 vols., Romae: Apud Aedes Universitatis Gregorianae, 1923-1938.

Woywod, Stanislaus, *A Practical Commentary on the Code of Canon Law,* 4. ed., 2 vols., New York: Wagner, 1932.

Periodicals

Apollinaris, Romae, 1928—

Collationes Brugenses, Brugis Flandrorum, 1895—

Commentarium Pro Religiosis (later *Commentarium Pro Religiosis et Missionariis*), Romae, 1920—

Homiletic and Pastoral Review, The, New York, 1900—

Jurist, The, Washington, 1941—

Jus Pontificium, Romae, 1921—

Le Canoniste (originally *Le Canoniste Contemporain,* 45 vols., Paris, 1878-1922), Vols. 46-48, 1924-1926.

Monitore Ecclesiastico, Il, Romae, 1876—

Periodica de Re Canonica et Morali utili Praesertim Religiosis et Missionariis, Bruges, 1905—

Abbreviations

AAS—Acta Apostolicae Sedis.

CpRM—Commentarium pro Religiosis et Missionariis.

Fontes—Codicis Iuris Canonici Fontes cura ... Gasparri editi.

Periodica—Periodica de Re Canonica et Morali Utili Praesertim Religiosis et Missionariis.

Schemata—Codicis Iuris Canonici Schemata ... I, De Iudiciis in Genere.

ALPHABETICAL INDEX

BIOGRAPHICAL NOTE

Michael James Keene was born on November 30, 1912, at Indianapolis, Indiana. After completing his elementary and secondary education, he entered the novitiate of the Benedictine Abbey of St. Meinrad, Indiana, August 5, 1931. After his religious profession, August 6, 1932, he made his philosophical and theological studies at St. Meinrad's Major Seminary. He was ordained to the priesthood after his third year of theology, May 18, 1937. After completing his fourth year of theology at the Pontifical Institute of St. Anselm in Rome, he matriculated in the school of Canon Law at the Pontifical Institute of Both Laws in Rome, November 1, 1938, where he received the degree of the Baccalaureate in Canon Law in July, 1939. In June of 1941 he received the Licentiate in Canon Law at the Catholic University of America.

CANON LAW STUDIES

1. Freriks, Rev. Celestine A., C.PP.S., J.C.D., Religious Congregations in Their External Relations, 121 pp., 1916.
2. Galliher, Rev. Daniel M., O.P., J.C.D., Canonical Elections, 117 pp., 1917.
3. Borkowski, Rev. Aurelius L., O.F.M., J.C.D., De Confraternitatibus Ecclesiasticis, 136 pp., 1918.
4. Castillo, Rev. Cayo, J.C.D., Disertacion Historico-Canonica sobre la Potestad del Cabildo en Sede Vacante o Impedida del Vicario Capitular, 99 pp., 1919 (1918).
5. Kubelbeck, Rev. William J., S.T.B., J.C.D., The Sacred Penitentiaria and its Relations to Faculties of Ordinaries and Priests, 129 pp., 1918.
6. Petrovits, Rev. Joseph J.C., S.T.D., J.C.D., The New Church Law On Matrimony, X-461 pp., 1919.
7. Hickey, Rev. John J., S.T.B., J.C.D., Irregularities and Simple Impediments in the New Code of Canon Law, 100 pp., 120.
8. Klekotka, Rev. Peter J., S.T.B., J.C.D., Diocesan Consultors, 179 pp., 1920.
9. Wanenmacher, Rev. Francis, J.C.D., The Evidence in Ecclesiastical Procedure Affecting the Marriage Bond, 1920 (Printed 1935).
10. Golden, Rev. Henry Francis, J.C.D., Parochial Benefices in the New Code, IV-119 pp., 1921 (Printed 1925).
11. Koudelka, Rev. Charles J., J.C.D., Pastors, Their Rights and Duties According to the New Code of Canon Law, 211 pp., 1921.
12. Melo, Rev. Antonius, O.F.M., J.C.D., De Exemptione Regularium, X-188 pp., 1921.
13. Schaaf, Rev. Valentine Theodore, O.F.M., S.T.B., J.C.D., The Cloister, X-180 pp., 1921.
14. Burke, Rev. Thomas Joseph, S.T.D., J.C.D., Competence in Ecclesiastical Tribunals, IV-117 pp., 1922.
15. Leech, Rev. George Leo, J.C.D., A Comparative Study of the Constitution, "Apostolicae Sedis" and the "Codex Juris Canonici," 179 pp., 1922.
16. Motry, Rev. Hubert Louis, S.T.D., J.C.D., Diocesan Faculties According to the Code of Canon Law, II-167 pp., 1922.
17. Murphy, Rev. George Lawrence, J.C.D., Delinquencies and Penalties in the Administration and Reception of the Sacraments, IV-121 pp., 1923.
18. O'Reilly, Rev. John Anthony, S.T.B., J.C.D., Ecclesiastical Sepulture in the New Code of Canon Law, II-129 pp., 1923.

19. Michalicka, Rev. Wenceslas Cyrill, O.S.B., J.C.D., Judicial Procedure in Dismissal of Clerical Exempt Religious, 107 pp., 1923.
20. Dargin, Rev. Edward Vincent, S.T.B., J.C.D., Reserved Cases According to the Code of Canon Law, IV-103, pp., 1924.
21. Godfrey, Rev. John A., S.T.B., J.C.D., The Right of Patronage According to the Code of Canon Law, 153 pp., 1924.
22. Hagedorn, Rev. Francis Edward, J.C.D., General Legislation on Indulgences, II-154 pp., 1924.
23. King, Rev. James Ignatius, J.C.D., The Administration of the Sacraments to Dying Non-Catholics, V-141 pp., 1924.
24. Winslow, Rev. Francis Joseph, M.M., J.C.D., Vicars and Prefects Apostolic, IV-149 pp., 1924.
25. Correa, Rev. Jose Servelion, S.T.L., J.C.D., La Potestad Legislativa de la Iglesia Catolica, IV-127 pp., 1925.
26. Dugan, Rev. Henry Francis, A.M., J.C.D., The Judiciary Department of the Diocesan Curia, 87 pp., 1925.
27. Keller, Rev. Charles Frederick, S.T.B., J.C.D., Mass Stipends, 167 pp., 1925.
28. Paschang, Rev. John Linus, J.C.D., The Sacramentals According to the Code of Canon Law, 129 pp., 1925.
29. Pointek, Rev. Cyrillus, O.F.M., S.T.B., J.C.D., De Indulto Exclaustrationis necnon Saecularizationis, XIII-289 pp., 1925.
30. Kearney, Rev. Richard Joseph, S.T.B., J.C.D., Sponsors at Baptism According to the Code of Canon Law, IV-127 pp., 1925.
31. Bartlett, Rev. Chester Joseph, A.M., LL.B., J.C.D., The Tenure of Parochial Property in the United States of America, V-108 pp., 1926.
32. Kilker, Rev. Adrian Jerome, J.C.D., Extreme Unction, V-425 pp., 1926.
33. McCormick, Rev. Robert Emmett, J.C.D., Confessors of Religious, VIII-266 pp., 1926.
34. Miller, Rev. Newton Thomas, J.C.D., Founded Masses According to the Code of Canon Law, VII-93 pp., 1926.
35. Roelker, Rev. Edward G., S.T.D., J.C.D., Principles of Privilege According to the Code of Canon Law, XI-166 pp., 1926.
36. Bakalarczyk, Rev. Richardus, M.I.C., J.U.D., De Novitiatu, VIII-208 pp., 1927.
37. Pizzuti, Rev. Lawrence, O.F.M., J.U.L., De Parochis Religiosis, 1927. (Not printed).
38. Bliley, Rev. Nicholas Martin, O.S.B., J.C.D., Altars According to the Code of Canon Law, XIX-132 pp., 1927.
39. Brown, Mr. Brendan Francis, A.B., LL.M., J.U.D., The Canonical Juristic Personality with Special Reference to Its Status in the United States of America, V-212 pp., 1927.

40. Cavanaugh, Rev. William Thomas, C.P., J.U.D., The Reservation of the Blessed Sacrament, VIII-101 pp., 1927.
41. Doheny, Rev. William J., C.S.C., A.B., J.U.D., Church Property: Modes of Acquisition, X-118 pp., 1927.
42. Feldhaus, Rev. Aloysius H., C.PP.S., J.C.D., Oratories, IX-141 pp., 1927.
43. Kelly, Rev. James Patrick, A.B., J.C.D., The Jurisdiction of the Simple Confessor, X-208 pp., 1927.
44. Neuberger, Rev. Nicholas J., J.C.D., Canon 6 or the Relation of the Codex Juris Canonici to the Preceding Legislation, V-95 pp., 1927.
45. O'Keefe, Rev. Gerald Michael, J.C.D., Matrimonial Dispensations, Powers of Bishop, Priests and Confessors, VIII-232 pp., 1927.
46. Quigley, Rev. Joseph A.M., A.B., J.C.B., Condemned Societies, 139 pp., 1927.
47. Zaplotnik, Rev. Johannes Leo, J.C.D., De Vicariis Foraneis, X-142 pp., 1927.
48. Duskie, Rev. John Aloysius, A.B., J.C.D., The Canonical Status of the Orientals in the United States, VIII-196 pp., 1928.
49. Hyland, Rev. Francis Edward, J.C.D., Excommunication, Its Nature, Historical Development and Effects, VIII-181 pp., 1928.
50. Reinmann, Rev. Gerald Joseph, O.M.C., J.C.D., The Third Order Secular of Saint Francis, 201 pp., 1928.
51. Schenk, Rev. Francis J., J.C.D., The Matrimonial Impediments of Mixed Religion and Disparity of Cult, XVI-318 pp., 1929.
52. Coady, Rev. John Joseph, S.T.D., J.U.D., A.M., The Appointment of Pastors, VIII-150 pp., 1929.
53. Kay, Rev. Thomas Henry, J.C.D., Competence in Matrimonial Procedure, VIII-164 pp., 1929.
54. Turner, Rev. Sidney Joseph, C.P., J.U.D., The Vow of Poverty, XLIX-217 pp., 1929.
55. Kearney, Rev. Raymond A., A.B., S.T.D., J.C.D., The Principles of Delegation, VII-149 pp., 1929.
56. Conran, Rev. Edward James, A.B., J.C.D., The Interdict, V-163 pp., 1930.
57. O'Neil, Rev. William H., J.C.D., Papal Rescripts of Favor, VII-218 pp., 1930.
58. Bastnagel, Rev. Clement Vincent, J.U.D., The Appointment of Parochial Adjutants and Assistants, XV-257 pp., 1930.
59. Ferry, Rev. William A., A.B., J.C.D., Stole Fees, V-135 pp., 1930.
60. Costello, Rev. John Michael, A.B., J.C.D., Domicile and Quasi-domicile, VII-201 pp., 1930.
61. Kremer, Rev. Michael Nicholas, A.B., S.T.B., J.C.D., Church Support in the United States, VI-136 pp., 1930.

62. Angulo, Rev. Luis, C.M., J.C.D., Legislation de la Iglesia sobre la intencion en la application de la Santa Misa, VII-104 pp., 1931.
63. Frey, Rev. Wolfgang Norbert, O.S.B., A.B., J.C.D., The Act of Religious Profession, VIII-174 pp., 1931.
64. Roberts, Rev. James Brendan, A.B., J.C.D., The Banns of Marriage, XIV-140 pp., 1931.
65. Ryder, Rev. Raymond Aloysius, A.B., J.C.D., Simony, IX-151 pp., 1931.
66. Campagna, Rev. Angelo, Ph.D., J.U.D., Il Vicario Generale del Vescovo, VII-205 pp., 1931.
67. Cox, Rev. Joseph Godfery, A.B., J.C.D., The Administration of Seminaries, VI-124 pp., 1931.
68. Gregory, Rev. Ronald J., J.U.D., The Pauline Privilege, XV-165 pp., 1931.
69. Donohue, Rev. John F., J.C.D., The Impediment of Crime, VII-110 pp., 1931.
70. Dooley, Rev. Eugene A., O.M.I., J.C.D., Church Law On Sacred Relics, IX-143 pp., 1931.
71. Orth, Rev. Raymond Clement, O.M.C., J.C.D., The Approbation of Religious Institutes, 171 pp., 1931.
72. Pernicone, Rev. Joseph M., A.B., J.C.D., The Ecclesiastical Prohibition of Books, XII-267 pp., 1932.
73. Clinton, Rev. Connell, A.B., J.C.D., The Paschal Precept, IX-108 pp., 1932.
74. Donnelly, Rev. Francis B., A.M., S.T.L., J.C.D., The Diocesan Synod, VIII-125 pp., 1932.
75. Torrente, Rev. Camilo, C.M.F., J.C.D., Las Processiones Sagradas, V-145 pp., 1932.
76. Murphy, Rev. Edwin J., C.PP.S., J.C.D., Suspension Ex Informata Conscientia, XI-122, pp., 1932.
77. Mackenzie, Rev. Eric F., A.M., S.T.L., J.C.D., The Delict of Heresy in its Commission, Penalization, Absolution, VII-124 pp., 1932.
78. Lyons, Rev. Avitus E., S.T.B., J.C.D., The Collegiate Tribunal of First Instance, XI-147 pp., 1932.
79. Connolly, Rev. Thomas A., J.C.D., Appeals, XI-195 pp., 1932.
80. Sangmeister, Rev. Joseph V., A.B., J.C.D., Force and Fear as Precluding Matrimonial Consent, V-211 pp., 1932.
81. Jaeger, Rev. Leo A., A.B., J.C.D., The Administration of Vacant and Quasi-vacant Episcopal Sees in the United States, IX-229 pp., 1932.
82. Rimlinger, Rev. Herbert T., J.C.D., Error Invalidating Matrimonial Consent, VII-79 pp., 1932.

83. Barrett, Rev. John D.M., S.S., J.C.D., A Comparative Study of the Third Plenary Council of Baltimore and the Code, IX-221 pp., 1932.
84. Carberry, Rev. John J., Ph.D., S.T.D., J.C.D., The Juridical Form of Marriage, X-177 pp., 1934.
85. Dolan, Rev. John L., A.B., J.C.D., The Defensor Vinculi, XII-157 pp., 1934.
86. Hannan, Rev. Jerome D., A.M., S.T.D., LL.B., J.C.D., The Canon Law of Wills, IX-517 pp., 1934.
87. Lemieux, Rev. Delisle A., A.M., J.C.D., The Sentence in Ecclesiastical Procedure, IX-131 pp., 1934.
88. O'Rourke, Rev. James J., A.B., J.C.D., Parish Registers, VII-109 pp., 1934.
89. Timlin, Rev. Bartholomew, O.F.M., A.M., J.C.D., Conditional Matrimonial Consent, X-381 pp., 1934.
90. Wahl, Rev. Francis X., A.B., J.C.D., The Matrimonial Impediments of Consanguinity and Affinity, VI-125 pp., 1934.
91. White, Rev. Robert J., A.B., LL.B., S.T.B., J.C.D., Canonical Ante-Nuptial Promises and the Civil Law, VI-152 pp., 1934.
92. Herrera, Rev. Antonio Parra, O.C.D., J.C.D., Legislation Ecclesiastica sobra el Ayuno y la Abstinencia, XI-191 pp., 1935.
93. Kennedy, Rev. Edwin J., J.C.D., The Special Matrimonial Process in Cases of Evident Nullity, X-165 pp., 1935.
94. Manning, Rev. John J., A.B., J.C.D., Presumption of Law in Matrimonial Procedure, XI-111 pp., 1935.
95. Moeder, Rev. John M., J.C.D., The Proper Bishop for Ordination and Dismissorial Letters, VII-135 pp., 1935.
96. O'Mara, Rev. William A., A.B., J.C.D., Canonical Causes For Matrimonial Dispensations, IX-155 pp., 1935.
97. Reilly, Rev. Peter, J.C.D., Residence of Pastors, IX-81 pp., 1935.
98. Smith, Rev. Mariner T., O.P., S.T.L., J.C.D., The Penal Law For Religious, VII-169 pp,, 1935.
99. Whalen, Rev. Donald W., A.M., J.C.D., The Value of Testimonial Evidence in Matrimonial Procedure, XIII-297 pp., 1935.
100. Cleary, Rev. Joseph F., J.C.D., Canonical Limitations on the Alienation of Church Property, VIII-141 pp., 1936.
101. Glynn, Rev. John C., J.C.D., The Promoter of Justice, XX-337 pp., 1936.
102. Brennan, Rev. James H., S.S., A.M., S.T.B., J.C.D., The Simple Convalidation of Marriage, VI-135 pp., 1937.
103. Brunini, Rev. Joseph Bernard, J.C.D., The Clerical Obligations of Canons 139 and 142, X-121 pp., 1937.
104. Connor, Rev. Maurice, A.B., J.C.D., The Administrative Removal of Pastors, VIII-159 pp., 1937.
105. Guilfoyle, Rev. Merlin Joseph, J.C.D., Custom, XI-144 pp., 1937.

106. Hughes, Rev. James Austin, A.B., A.M., J.C.D., Witnesses in Criminal Trials of Clerics, IX-140 pp., 1937.
107. Jansen, Rev. Raymond J., A.B., S.T.L., J.C.D., Canonical Provisions for Catechetical Instruction, VII-153 pp., 1937.
108. Kealy, Rev. John James, A.B., J.C.D., The Introductory Libellus in Church Court Procedure, XI-121 pp., 1937.
109. McManus, Rev. James Edward, C.SS.R., J.C.D., The Administration of Temporal Goods in Religious Institutes, XVI-196 pp., 1937.
110. Moriarty, Rev. Eugene James, J.C.D., Oaths in Ecclesiastical Courts, X-115 pp., 1937.
111. Rainer, Rev. Eligius George, C.SS.R., J.C.D., Suspension of Clerics, XVII-249 pp., 1937.
112. Reilly, Rev. Thomas F., C.SS.R., J.C.D., Visitation of Religious, VI-195 pp., 1938.
113. Moriarty, Rev. Francis E., C.SS.R., J.C.D., The Extraordinary Absolution from Censures, XV-334 pp., 1938.
114. Connolly, Rev. Nicholas P., J.C.D., The Canonical Erection of Parishes, X-132 pp., 1938.
115. Donovan, Rev. James Joseph, J.C.D., The Pastor's Obligation in Prenuptial Investigation, XII-322 pp., 1938.
116. Harrigan, Rev. Robert J., M.A., S.T.B., J.C.D., The Radical Sanation of Invalid Marriages, VIII-208 pp., 1938.
117. Boffa, Rev. Conrad Humbert, J.C.D., Canonical Provisions for Catholic Schools, X-211 pp., 1939.
118. Parsons, Rev. Anscar John, O.M. Cap., J.C.D., Canonical Elections, XII-236 pp., 1939.
119. Reilly, Rev. Edward Michael, A.B., J.C.D., The General Norms of Dispensation, X-156, pp., 1939.
120. Ryan, Rev. Gerald Aloysius, A.B., J.C.D., Principles of Episcopal Jurisdiction, XII-172 pp., 1939.
121. Burton, Rev. Francis James, C.S.C., A.B., J.C.D., A Commentary on Canon 1125, X-222 pp., 1940.
122. Miaskiewicz, Rev. Francis Sigismund, J.C.D., Supplied Jurisdiction according to Canon 209, XII-340 pp., 1940.
123. Rice, Rev. Patrick William, A.B., J.C.D., Proof of Death in Prenuptial Investigation, VIII-156 pp., 1940.
124. Anglin, Rev. Thomas Francis, M.S., J.C.L., The Eucharistic Fast.
125. Coleman, Rev. John Jerome, J.C.L., The Minister of Confirmation.
126. Downs, Rev. John Emmanuel, A.B., J.C.L., The Concept of Clerical Immunity.
127. Esswein, Rev. Anthony Albert, J.C.L., Extrajudicial Penal Powers of Ecclesiastical Superiors.

128. Farrell, Rev. Benjamin Francis, M.A., S.T.L., J.C.L., The Rights and Duties of the Local Ordinary Regarding Congregations of Women Religious of Pontifical Approval.
129. Feeney, Rev. Thomas John, A.B., S.T.L., J.C.L., Restitutio in Integrum.
130. Findlay, Rev. Stephen William, O.S.B., A.B., J.C.L., Canonical Norms Governing the Deposition and Degradation of Clerics.
131. Goodwine, Rev. John, A. B., S.T.L., The Right of the Church to Acquire Property.
132. Heston, Rev. Edward Louis, C.S.C., Ph.D., S.T.D., J.C.L., The Alienation of Church Property in the United States.
133. Hogan, Rev. James John, S.T.L., J.C.L., Judicial Advocates and Procurators.
134. Kealy, Rev. Thomas M., A.B., Litt. B., J.C.L., Dowry of Women Religious.
135. Keene, Rev. Michael James, O.S.B., J.C.L., Religious Ordinaries and Canon 198.
136. Kerin, Rev. Charles A., S.S., M.A., S.T.B., J.C.L., The Privation of Christian Burial.
137. Louis, Rev. William Francis, M.A., J.C.L., Diocesan Archives.
138. McDevitt, Rev. Gilbert Joseph, A.B., J.C.L., Legitimacy and Legitimation.
139. McDonough, Rev. Thomas Joseph, A.B., J.C.L., Apostolic Administrators.
140. Meier, Rev. Carl Anthony, A.B., J.C.L., Penal Administrative Procedure Against Negligent Pastors.
141. Schmidt, Rev. John Rogg, A.B., J.C.L., The Principles of Authentic Interpretation in Canon 17 of the Code of Canon Law.
142. Slafkosky, Rev. Andrew Leonard, A.B., J.C.L., The Canonical Episcopal Visitation of the Diocese.
143. Swoboda, Rev. Innocent Robert, O.F.M., J.C.L., Ignorance in Relation to the Imputability of Delicts.
144. Dubé, Rev. Arthur Joseph, A.B., J.C.L., The General Principles for the Reckoning of Time in Canon Law.
145. McBride, Rev. T., A.B., J.C.L., Incardination and Excardination of Seculars.

www.ingramcontent.com/pod-product-compliance
Lightning Source LLC
LaVergne TN
LVHW050228080826
844660LV00012B/497

9780813223247